INTERMEDIATE LEVEL
NVQ/SVQ 3

Unit 7

Preparing Reports and Returns

WORKBOOK

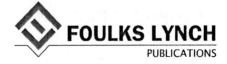

FOULKS LYNCH
PUBLICATIONS

British Library Cataloguing-in-Publication Data

A catalogue record for this book is available from the British Library.

Published by

Foulks Lynch Ltd
4, The Griffin Centre
Staines Road
Feltham
Middlesex
TW14 0HS

ISBN 0 7483 5951 6

Printed and Bound in Great Britain

© Foulks Lynch Ltd, 2003

Acknowledgments

We are grateful to the Association of Accounting Technicians for permission to reproduce the 2003 specimen simulation and for permission to reproduce expired simulations. The answers to expired simuations have been prepared by Foulks Lynch.

CONTENTS

FOULKS LYNCH
PUBLICATIONS

INTRODUCTION

This is the new edition of the AAT Workbook for Unit 7 – *Preparing Reports and Returns*.

Tailored to the new standards of competence, this workbook has been written specifically for AAT students in a clear and comprehensive style.

This workbook contains numerous practice activities, to reinforce the main topics you will need to prove your competence in. It also includes the specimen simulation released by the AAT, which shows the kind questions you will be faced with in your AAT simulation. In addition, there are six further simulations covering various performance criteria for plently of practice before your actual assessment.

ASSESSMENT

Unit 7 is assessed by means of **Skills Testing.**

Skills testing when your approved assessment centre (AAC) is a workplace

You may be observed carrying out your accounting activities as part of your normal work routine. You need to collect documentary evidence of the work you have done in an accounting portfolio.

Skills testing when your AAC is a college

This will use a combination of:

- documentary evidence of activities carried out at work, collected in a portfolio
- realistic simulations of workplace activities
- projects and assignments.

Skills testing when you don't work in accountancy

Don't worry – you can prove your competence using one of AAT's simulations, or from case studies, projects and assignments.

The AAT simulation

- Each simulation will be three hours long, with an additional 15 minutes reading time.
- Each simulation will be based around a single scenario containing information relevant to all three elements of the unit.
- There will be **no** question of you having to calculate minority interests, goodwill on consolidation or any of the other special techniques associated with group accounts.
- Typically you will be presented with profit and loss accounts, balance sheets or similar financial statements and are asked to consolidate them and then to calculate ratios etc.
- You will **not** have to deal with unrealised profit.
- You will **always** be required to prepare a report on some aspect of the figures presented.
- You will usually be required to complete a standard form prepared by an external agency. The form will always refer to the consolidated figures, never to the figures relating to individual organisational units.
- You will invariably be required to complete a VAT return.
- There may also be instances where actual invoices or similar documents (e.g. a proforma invoice) are presented, and you will be required to determine whether or not it is appropriate to account for the related VAT.

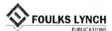

PRACTICE ACTIVITIES

BASIC MATHEMATICAL TECHNIQUES

ACTIVITY 1

Task

Calculate a weighted average of the following prices, using the quantities sold as weights:

Price (£)	Quantity sold
10	50
12	100
14	40
16	20

ACTIVITY 2

A contribution statement has been produced for two products manufactured by Xtra Ltd.

	Product A Budget £	Product B Actual £	% Change	Budget £	Actual £	% Change
Sales	98,000	103,000		14,000	20,000	
Material costs	(34,000)	(39,000)		(4,600)	(7,200)	
Labour costs	(24,200)	(23,600)		(2,650)	(2,650)	
Overheads	(24,200)	(20,000)		(2,650)	(3,400)	
Contribution	15,600	20,400		4,100	6,750	

Task

Show the percentage changes in the columns provided.

TABULATION OF DATA

ACTIVITY 3

Alpha Products plc has two departments, A and B. The total wage bill in 20X7 was £513,000, of which £218,000 was for department A and the rest for department B. The corresponding figures for 20X8 were £537,000 and £224,000. The number employed in department A was 30 in 20X7 and decreased by five for the next year. The number employed in department B was 42 in 20X7 and increased by one for the year 20X8.

Task

Tabulate this data to bring out the changes over the two-year period for each department and the company as a whole.

ACTIVITY 4

The following information has been provided by Waterson plc:

In the property division, for the year ended 31 March 20X9, pre-tax profits were £15,426,000 compared with £12,141,000 for the previous year. Earnings per share were 29.62 pence, compared with 24.10 pence in the previous year, and dividends per share were 13.50 pence compared with 11.52 pence for the previous year.

In the manufacturing division for the same periods, pre-tax profits were £9,271,000 compared with £8,343,000, earnings per share were 15.75 pence compared with 14.91 pence, and dividends were 9.63 pence per share compared with 8.86 pence.

Task 1

Put this data into tabular form, and include in your table the proportion of total group profits earned by each division in each year.

ACTIVITY 5

Fifty male university students were selected at random and their heights were measured in centimetres. The following values were found and recorded:

174	196	179	181	193
179	186	182	170	182
170	193	181	180	181
182	179	187	169	186
168	182	176	169	181
187	191	167	190	187
191	178	180	194	197
186	179	181	176	195
179	170	180	190	182
199	169	180	183	180

Task

Using the data given, construct a grouped frequency distribution of the university students' heights.

ACTIVITY 6

The price of the ordinary 25p shares of Manco plc quoted on the London Stock Exchange at the close of business on successive Fridays is tabulated below:

126	120	122	105	129	119	131	138
125	127	113	112	130	122	134	136
128	126	117	114	120	123	127	140
124	127	114	111	116	131	128	137
127	122	106	121	116	135	142	130

Task

Group the above data into eight classes.

ACTIVITY 7

The United Kingdom's merchant shipping fleet of vessels of 500 gross tonnes and over in April 20X5 consisted of:

Type	Number of vessels	Gross tonnage ('000)
Passenger vessels	85	626
Tankers	257	6,812
Cargo liners	97	876
Container vessels	55	1,559
Tramps	167	352
Bulk carriers	80	3,109

In April 20X3, the figures were:

Passenger vessels	86	573
Tankers	329	10,030
Cargo liners	134	1,194
Container vessels	64	1,613
Tramps	190	406
Bulk carriers	128	4,709

Task

Set out the foregoing information in the form of a table. The required table format is as follows:

	Number of vessels				Gross tonnage (000)			
			Change				Change	
	20X3	20X5	Actual	%	20X3	20X5	Actual	%
Type of vessel								
Total								

DIAGRAMMATIC PRESENTATION

ACTIVITY 8

For the years 20X6 and 20X7 an analysis of sales by market is given as:

	Sales in 20X6 £'000	Sales in 20X7 £'000
United Kingdom	1,760	1,800
EC countries (other than UK)	576	612
Other European countries	214	374
North and South America	306	354
CIS	54	72
Other overseas countries	127	584

Task

Draw comparative pie charts illustrating the figures given for each year.

Show your workings.

ACTIVITY 9

The following data has been extracted from the annual report of a manufacturing company:

	Annual sales	(£ million)
	20X8	20X7
United Kingdom	35.0	31.5
EC (other than UK)	47.4	33.2
North America	78.9	40.3
Australia	18.2	26.1

Task

Represent this data by component bar charts.

ACTIVITY 10

A department store has three departments, as listed below, together with the sales for the years 20X5, 20X6 and 20X7.

	Sales (£'000,000)		
Department	20X5	20X6	20X7
Furnishing	5	6	8
Clothing	12	15	19
Hardware	3	4	4

Task

Construct multiple bar charts to represent the data over the three years.

ACTIVITY 11

The management of an industrial company wants to supply financial information to its employees in chart form.

The following information for the five years from 20X1 to 20X5 inclusive is available:

Year	20X5	20X4	20X3	20X2	20X1
	£m	£m	£m	£m	£m
Sales	6.3	6.5	5.8	4.7	3.9
Direct materials	3.1	3.2	2.8	2.2	1.9
Direct wages	1.4	1.2	1.1	1.0	0.8
Production overhead	1.0	1.0	0.9	0.8	0.6
Other overhead	0.4	0.4	0.3	0.2	0.2
Taxation	0.3	0.3	0.3	0.2	0.2
Profit	0.1	0.4	0.4	0.3	0.2

Product groups:

% of total sales	%	%	%	%	%
Product A	24	22	20	20	15
B	12	10	11	9	12
C	16	21	23	26	30
Other products	48	47	46	45	43
	100	100	100	100	100

Tasks

1   As management accountant, prepare for the managing director a component bar chart (supported by any necessary calculation) to show sales by product groups.

2   Using the data given in (1), prepare 2 pie charts showing costs, taxation and profit for 20X4 and 20X5 with particular emphasis on direct wages.

3   What do the two pie charts tell you about the performance over the two years?

GRAPHICAL PRESENTATION

ACTIVITY 12

The AT Photographic Company's sales of its Space Age camera for the two years 20X7/20X8 and 20X8/20X9 were as follows:

	20X7/20X8	20X8/20X9
June	562	705
July	514	624
August	648	582
September	566	711
October	743	862
November	816	1,027
December	863	963
January	627	706
February	428	531
March	558	664
April	564	713
May	811	912

Task

Round each month's sales to the nearest hundred and use this data to prepare a Z chart for 20X8/20X9.

ACTIVITY 13

A sample of 12 packets taken from an automatic filling machine had the following weights in kilograms:

504, 506, 501, 505, 507, 506, 504, 508, 503, 505, 502, 504

Task

Find:

(a) The median weight.

(b) The modal weight.

(c) The arithmetic mean weight.

ACTIVITY 14

In preparing a report on advertising costs for a proposed new newspaper, the following information was collated about newspapers already in circulation:

Newspaper	Circulation (millions)	Advertising rate per page (£'000)
A	4.08	21.9
B	3.49	21.3
C	2.00	14.7
D	1.86	14.5
E	1.63	8.6
F	0.77	6.3
G	0.49	6.0

Tasks

1   Plot the data on a scatter graph.

2   Fit, by eye, a straight line to the points.

3   Use the line to estimate a suitable advertising rate for the new newspaper which is expected to have a circulation of one million.

ACTIVITY 15

The times taken (in minutes) by 35 employees in a factory to complete an operation are as follows:

5.6	6.9	4.3	6.8	6.3
8.9	3.1	5.6	7.3	8.4
4.6	4.1	3.8	6.2	7.5
3.8	2.1	4.7	5.6	6.1
5.4	6.2	5.1	5.6	7.5
5.7	2.8	5.4	9.0	5.1
8.3	7.9	5.8	4.2	1.7

Tasks

1   Present the data in the form of a grouped frequency table.

2   Present the data in the form of a histogram,

ACTIVITY 16

Task

The average speed of 100 cars was recorded on a dangerous section of road.

From the following data prepare:

1   a histogram; and

2   a frequency polygon

Speed of cars mph	Number of cars
≥ 60 < 63	5
≥ 63 < 66	18
≥ 66 < 69	42
≥ 69 < 72	27
≥ 72 < 75	8
	___
	100
	___

ACTIVITY 17

The following table shows the heights of a sample of 100 cabinets. Calculate the arithmetic mean.

Class interval Height (cms)	Frequency f
≥ 150 < 160	1
≥ 160 < 170	9
≥ 170 < 180	12
≥ 180 < 190	16
≥ 190 < 200	26
≥ 200 < 210	19
≥ 210 < 220	8
≥ 220 < 230	6
≥ 230 < 240	2
≥ 240 < 250	1
	Sum of f = 100

ACTIVITY 18

The following data describes the length of time, in minutes, taken by 60 employees in the accounts section of P Ltd using photocopier X during the course of a typical working day:

1.2	10.1	7.3	3.1	8.4	3.7	1.4	6.6	5.1	6.0
5.7	0.5	6.2	2.4	4.5	4.8	2.7	4.9	9.2	6.2
4.3	11.4	6.5	5.0	3.9	9.0	11.6	5.7	10.9	7.4
1.9	8.6	9.1	1.9	5.1	6.3	3.9	7.0	8.6	5.7
3.4	7.2	0.8	6.8	7.6	6.9	4.8	8.9	4.9	5.3
2.9	1.6	3.4	10.7	6.0	7.4	5.2	4.5	5.8	8.1

Tasks

1   Form these data into a frequency distribution of six classes and comment upon its shape.

2   Draw, on graph paper, the histogram of this frequency distribution.

3   What is the modal class and what does this tell us? Explain your result clearly.

4   Calculate the mean of the frequency distribution.

TIME SERIES ANALYSIS

ACTIVITY 19

A domestic appliance retailer offers customers the chance to purchase an insurance policy to cover the cost of repairs, if needed, over five years. The policy can only be purchased when the appliance is first purchased.

The following table shows the sales of appliances, together with the number of policies sold, over the period 20X1 to 20X7.

Year	Sales of appliances at 20X1 prices (£'000)	Sales of policies (number)
20X1	3,000	400
20X2	5,000	300
20X3	7,000	600
20X4	10,000	1,200
20X5	15,000	1,700
20X6	18,000	2,200
20X7	19,000	2,000

Tasks

1   Plot a scatter graph of sales of appliances against year and draw by eye the line of best fit.

2   By extrapolating the line, forecast appliance sales for 20X8 and 20X9.

3   Plot a scatter graph of policy sales against appliance sales and draw the line of best fit.

4   Use the line obtained in (c) and the forecast of sales in (b) to predict policy sales for 20X8 and 20X9. Comment on the reliability of your forecast.

ACTIVITY 20

State which type of time series component you would expect to be prominent in the following types of data:

(a)   Monthly sales of ice cream by a long established ice cream vendor.

(b)   Monthly sales of bread by a new bakery steadily increasing its market share.

(c)   Quarterly sales of Wellington boots by a long established manufacturer.

(d)   Annual passenger miles by an airline.

(e)   Sales of a staple product subject to obsolescence.

Volume of production per month from a factory where morale among the workforce is low, leading to frequent disputes, absenteeism and accidents.

ACTIVITY 21

The following are the sales figures for Bloggs Brothers Engineering Ltd for the 14 years from 20X1 to 20Y4:

Year	Sales £'000
20X1	491
20X2	519
20X3	407
20X4	452
20X5	607
20X6	681
20X7	764
20X8	696
20X9	751
20Y0	802
20Y1	970
20Y2	1,026
20Y3	903
20Y4	998

Task

Using the method of moving averages, establish the general trend of sales.

ACTIVITY 22

The daily output of Malcan plc over a four week period is shown in the table below:

	Monday	Tuesday	Wednesday	Thursday	Friday
Week 1	187	203	208	207	217
Week 2	207	208	210	206	212
Week 3	202	210	212	205	214
Week 4	208	215	217	217	213

Number of units of output

Tasks

1   Establish the five-period moving average trend of output.

2   Display on a graph the actual data together with the trend figures.

INDEX NUMBERS

ACTIVITY 23

Task

Given the following prices and sale quantities for a model of refrigerator sold by an electrical wholesaler, calculate price and quantity relatives for 20X2 and 20X3 with 20X1 as base. Comment on the results.

Sales of Model A refrigerator, 20X1 to 20X3

Year	Price	Sales
	£	'000
20X1	120	5.3
20X2	125	5.2
20X3	131	5.0

ACTIVITY 24

Below you will find the monthly values of an index appropriate to the industry in which Coleman Limited operates. The monthly values are relative to a base figure of 100, being the value of the index in January 2000.

You are required to calculate the indexed value of the monthly sales, in January 2000 terms, for each month's sales in 2003.

Index base = 100 (January 2000)

		Index	Sales £'000
2003	January	110.5	366
	February	109.8	228
	March	110.8	229
	April	111.2	316
	May	111.4	308
	June	111.7	284
	July	111.5	222
	August	111.6	342
	September	111.9	330
	October	112.0	292
	November	112.3	266
	December	112.7	358

ACTIVITY 25

A shopkeeper received the following amounts from the sale of radios:

20X1	£1,000
20X2	£1,100
20X3	£1,210
20X4	£1,331
20X5	£1,464

Task

By using chain base indices, decide whether it is correct to say that the annual rate of increase of sales of radios is getting larger.

PERFORMANCE INDICATORS

ACTIVITY 26

You are presented with the following summarised information concerning J Free:

Trading, profit and loss account (extracts)
for the year to 30 April 20X2 and 30 April 20X3

	20X3	20X2
	£	£
Sales (all on credit)	200,000	120,000
Cost of sales	(150,000)	(80,000)
Gross profit	50,000	40,000
Expenses	(15,000)	(10,000)
Net profit	35,000	30,000

Balance sheet (extracts) at 30 April 20X2 and 30 April 20X3

	20X3		20X2	
	£	£	£	£
Fixed assets (net book value)		12,000		15,000
Current assets				
Stocks	18,000		7,000	
Trade debtors	36,000		12,000	
Cash at bank	–		1,000	
		54,000		20,000
		66,000		35,000

FOULKS LYNCH
PUBLICATIONS

Capital account

Balance at 1 April	29,000		12,000	
Net profit for the year	35,000		30,000	
	64,000		42,000	
Less: Drawings	(23,000)		(13,000)	
		41,000		29,000
Current liabilities				
Trade creditors	15,000		6,000	
Bank overdraft	10,000		–	
		25,000		6,000
		66,000		35,000

Notes

(1)   There were no purchases or disposals of fixed assets during the year.

(2)   During 20X2/20X3 Free reduced his selling prices in order to stimulate sales.

(3)   It may be assumed that price levels were stable.

Tasks

1   Calculate the following ratios for both 20X2 and 20X3:

   (i)   net profit on sales;

   (ii)   gross profit on sales;

   (iii)   return on capital employed;

   (iv)   debtor collection period;

   (v)   current ratio; and

   (vi)   acid test (or quick) ratio.

2   State what changes appear to have arisen as a result of the reduction in selling prices.

ACTIVITY 27

The following extracts relate to K George's accounts for the year to 31 August 20X4:

Trading, profit and loss account for the year to 31 August 20X4

	£	£
Sales (all credit)		100,000
Less: Cost of goods sold		
Opening stock	10,000	
Purchases	52,000	
	62,000	
Less: Closing stock	(12,000)	
		(50,000)

Gross profit		50,000
Less: Expenses		(25,000)
		———
Net profit		25,000
		———

Balance sheet at 31 August 20X4

	£	£
Fixed assets		
Machinery at cost	30,000	
Less: Depreciation	(12,000)	
	———	
		18,000
Current assets		
Stocks	12,000	
Trade debtors	7,000	
Bank	1,000	
	———	
		20,000
Less: Current liabilities		
Trade creditors	5,000	
	———	
		(5,000)
		———
		33,000
		———
Financed by		
Capital		18,000
Net profit for the year		25,000
Less: Drawings		(10,000)
		———
		33,000
		———

Task

Calculate the following accounting ratios:

(a)　gross profit percentage;

(b)　net profit percentage;

(c)　return on capital employed;

(d)　stock turnover;

(e)　debtor collection period;

(f)　current ratio; and

(g)　quick (or acid test).

ACTIVITY 28

Total rail business		20X6/X7	20X7/X8	20X8/X9	20X9/Y0	20Y0/Y1
A to B Railway Company Ltd						
41 Total receipts per train mile	£	9.48	9.52	9.47	10.72	10.25
42 Total operating expenses per train mile	£	12.85	12.58	11.54	13.36	13.28
43 Train miles per member of staff (total staff productivity)	Miles	1,812	1,967	2,123	2,113	2,114
44 Revenue per £1,000 gross paybill costs	£	1,510	1,594	1,711	1,615	1,574
45 Train miles per train crew member (train crew productivity)	miles	8,564	9,568	10,485	10,727	10,961
46 Train miles per single track mile	'000	12.6	13.1	13.5	13.5	13.7

The above information has come from the accounts of A to B Railway Company Ltd.

Some of the indicators are partly based on financial data (41, 42 and 44). These have been adjusted to take account of changing price levels by converting each to 20Y0/Y1 price levels using the GDP deflator.

Task

For each of the performance indicators, briefly give your opinion on the success or otherwise of A to B Railway Company Ltd over the five-year period.

ACTIVITY 29

The following information is provided for a 30-day period for the rooms department of a hotel:

	Rooms with twin beds	Single rooms
Number of rooms in hotel	260	70
Number of rooms available to let	240	40
Average number of rooms occupied daily	200	30

Number of guests in period	6,450
Average length of stay	2 days
Total revenue in period	£774,000
Number of employees	200
Payroll costs for period	£100,000
Items laundered in period	15,000
Cost of cleaning supplies in period	£5,000
Total cost of laundering	£22,500
Listed daily rate for twin-bedded room	£110
Listed daily rate for single room	£70

The hotel calculates a number of statistics, including the following:

Room occupancy	Total number of rooms occupied as a percentage of rooms available to let
Bed occupancy	Total number of beds occupied as a percentage of beds available
Average guest rate	Total revenue divided by number of guests
Revenue utilisation	Actual revenue as a percentage of maximum revenue from available rooms
Average cost per occupied bed	Total cost divided by number of beds occupied

Task

Prepare a table which contains the following statistics, calculated to one decimal place:

(a)   room occupancy (%)

(b)   bed occupancy (%)

(c)   average guest rate (£)

(d)   revenue utilisation (%)

(e)   cost of cleaning supplies per occupied room per day (£)

(f)   average cost per occupied bed per day (£)

WRITING REPORTS

ACTIVITY 30

You are given the following information about Coleman Limited for 20X4.

Turnover	£3,541,000
Production cost	£2,070,000
Administration costs	£523,000
Distribution costs	£401,000
Total of all other costs	£151,000
Capital employed	£583,000
Number of units produced and sold	181,000
Average number of employees	117

Task

You are required to write a memo to the accounts supervisor, Roger Byrne, presenting the following ratios for his information:

• gross profit percentage

• net profit percentage

• production cost per unit produced

• value of sales per employee

Calculate ratios to two decimal places and monetary amounts to the nearest penny.

ACTIVITY 31

City Hotels Limited accountant has asked you to compare the performance of three hotels in the group over the last five years.

City Hotels Limited
Revenue from rooms let 20X2–20X6
All figures in £'000

	20X2	20X3	20X4	20X5	20X6
Station Hotel	£1,150	£1,250	£1,200	£1,250	£1,300
Airport Hotel	£1,250	£1,400	£2,300	£2,600	£2,750
Central Hotel	£850	£900	£850	£950	£1,100

Task

1   Using graph paper, prepare a clearly labelled line-graph showing the performance of each of the three hotels for the period 20X2–20X6.

A bar chart will not be acceptable.

2   Prepare a memo for the hotel accountant which should

- analyse the trends shown by the graph you have prepared

- mention any limitations in the trends shown by your analysis.

ACTIVITY 32

Super Shops is a business which sells sweets, chocolates and souvenirs from shops in the tourist areas of London. It currently rents four shops: North, South, East and West. It also rents a small office for central administration purposes.

You are the accounting technician employed to assist the owner, Manish Shah.

The following information is available to you:

Business Policy:

- all products are purchased centrally, therefore the purchase price is the same for products, regardless of which shop they are sold in;

- whilst the selling price of some products is controlled by the owner, the shop managers are free to reduce the price of other products to improve sales;

- central administration costs are shared equally between the four shops.

Super Shops

Profit and Loss Account for the year ended 31 March 20X3

	North	South	East	West	Total
	£	£	£	£	£
Sales	973,000	824,000	1,240,000	456,000	3,493,000
Less Cost of Goods sold	710,000	648,000	850,000	312,000	2,520,000
Gross Profit	263,000	176,000	390,000	144,000	973,000
Less expenses:					
Wages	48,000	42,000	102,000	20,000	212,000
Rent	128,000	92,000	153,000	67,000	440,000
Sundries	16,500	9,600	34,000	9,000	69,000
Share of Central Costs	45,000	45,000	45,000	45,000	180,000
	237,500	188,600	334,000	141,000	901,100
Net Profit	25,500	(12,600)	56,000	3,000	71,900

Notes:

- wages include the wages of the shop manager and shop assistants. The shop manager determines the number of shop assistants employed;

- sundries include any other costs incurred by the shop managers for the benefit of their shops. These include electricity, local advertising and cleaning.

Task 1

Complete the Performance Ratio Table below. Show all ratios to two decimal places.

Super Shops

Profit and Loss Account for the year ended 31 March 20X3

	North	South	East	West	Total
Gross Profit/Sales (%)					
Net Profit/Sales (%)					
Expense Ratios:					
Wages/Sales (%)	4.93	5.10	8.23	4.39	
Rent/Sales (%)	13.16	11.17	12.34	14.69	
Sundries/Sales (%)	1.70	1.17	2.74	1.97	
Central Costs/Sales (%)	4.62	5.46	3.63	9.87	

Task 2

Prepare a well-presented report for Mr Shah, comparing the performance of the four shops. You should address the following:

- gross profit/sales ratio;

- expense ratios (wages, rents sundries and central costs);

- overall net profitability of the shops;

- any limitations to your analysis.

Your report should relate the performance of individual shops to the other shops and to the business as a whole, offering explanations where you consider it appropriate. You should also consider the effect of business policy on the relative profitability of the shops.

INTRODUCTION TO VAT – SUPPLIES AND REGISTRATION

ACTIVITY 33

Calculate the VAT and gross price from the following net prices:

(a)   £216.00;

(b)   £5,926.00;

(c)   £11,144.00.

ACTIVITY 34

Calculate the VAT and net price from the following gross prices:

(a)   £715.81.

(b)   £1,292.50.

(c)   £7,336.23.

ACTIVITY 35

Su Chin makes cellos. In order to do so she has to buy wood. She has bought wood for one cello costing £1,000 on which she pays VAT at 17.5%. When she has produced the cello from this wood then she will sell it to a musical instrument dealer, Jake, for £3,000 plus VAT at 17.5% and he will sell it to a customer, the consumer, for £6,000 plus VAT at 17.5%.

How much VAT is paid to Customs & Excise by Su Chin and by Jake, and how much will the consumer pay for the cello?

ACTIVITY 36

A trader buys goods for £1,762.50 including VAT at 17.5% and sells them for £2,000 plus VAT at 17.5%. How much VAT does this trader pay to Customs & Excise?

ACTIVITY 37

Briefly explain the difference between exempt and zero-rated supplies, giving an example of each.

ACTIVITY 38

When is the basic tax point:

(a)   for goods

(b)   for services.

VAT INVOICES, VAT PERIODS, RECORDS REQUIRED

ACTIVITY 39

Consider the following invoice and comment upon whether or not it is a valid and correct tax invoice.

	XYZ Ltd
	123 Mount Place
	London
To: ABC Ltd	
789 St Johns Walk	
Birmingham	
23 July 20X7	
	£
Goods	2,160.00
VAT @ 17.5%	378.00
	2,538.00
Terms: 2% 30 days	
3% 10 days	
Net 60 days	

ACTIVITY 40

Consider the following invoice and comment upon whether or not it is a valid and correct tax invoice.

	All-u-want Ltd
	2 High Street
	Smallton
	SL1 1LM
	VAT No. 789 1234 56
Total	£82.99
(inclusive of VAT at the rate of ....%).	

ACTIVITY 41

A trader sells various articles for the following net amounts. What is the VAT and gross amount for each article?

(a)   £200

(b)   £1,300

(c)   £4,444

ACTIVITY 42

A trader sells various articles for the following gross amounts. What is the VAT and net for each article?

(a)   £117.03

(b)   £1,238.45

(c)   £7,153.87

(d)   £9,973.40

ACTIVITY 43

Goods are to be sold for £1,000 plus VAT at 17.5%. The terms of the sale are that a 3% cash discount is offered for payment within 10 days and a 2% discount for payment within 21 days.

What amounts would appear on the invoice for the sale of the goods and the VAT?

ACTIVITY 44

Calculate the VAT that would be charged on the following sale:

No	Item	Unit price
		£
5	Crates	10.05
8	Tubs	13.25
6	Barrels	15.15

A 5% cash discount is offered for settlement within 7 days.

ACTIVITY 45

Giles has been allocated prescribed accounting periods ending 28 February, 31 May, 31 August and 30 November.

What action should he take if:

(a)   His accounting year end is 31st March?

(b)   He expands his business abroad so that he will be due repayments of VAT?

ACTIVITY 46

John's financial year ends on 31 December 20X8. He uses the annual accounting scheme and had made three quarterly payments of £720 each. His total liability for the year is £3,820.

What return and payments must he make for the year, and what payments must he make for the following year?

ACTIVITY 47

Larry, a trader, keeps the following records:

(a)   A copy of the tax invoices he issues.

(b)   A list of the tax invoices in the order in which they are paid by the customer, showing the VAT and the VAT inclusive amount.

(c)   The tax invoices he receives (in no particular order).

(d)   A list of the purchase invoices in the order he pays them, showing the VAT and the VAT inclusive amount.

Larry pays VAT quarterly. The VAT account in the nominal ledger (ie, part of Larry's bookkeeping system) is completed by his accountant once a year. Larry makes no imports or exports.

Are Larry's records adequate?

COMPLETING THE VAT RETURN

ACTIVITY 48

Michael had issued the following incorrect tax invoices:

Invoice No	Gross	VAT	Net
	£	£	£
001	2,300	300	2,000
002	2,400	400	2,000

What should he do?

ACTIVITY 49

The following details were extracted from Stella's books for the 3 months to 31 May 20X7.

Purchases Day Book

	Description	Gross	VAT	Purchases	Expenses
		£	£	£	£
Mar	Total	21,150	3,150	16,000	2,000
Apr	Total	19,975	2,975	14,000	3,000
May	Total	18,800	2,800	14,000	2,000

Sales day book

	Description	Gross	VAT	Sales	Other
		£	£	£	£
Mar	Total	27,025	4,025	23,000	
Apr	Total	24,675	3,675	21,000	
May	Total	28,200	4,200	22,000	2,000

Note: office furniture was sold for £2,000 plus VAT in May.

Cash payments book

	Description	Gross	VAT	Purchases	Wages	Creditors
		£	£	£	£	£
Mar	Total	26,380	280	1,600	12,000	12,500
Apr	Total	28,320	420	2,400	12,500	13,000
May	Total	27,850	350	2,000	11,500	14,000

Cash receipts book

	Description	Gross	VAT	Sales	Debtors
		£	£	£	£
Mar	Total	22,850	350	2,000	20,500
Apr	Total	23,175	175	1,000	22,000
May	Total	23,350	350	2,000	21,000

Compute her outputs and output tax, and her inputs and input tax.

ACTIVITY 50

A trader provides the following information for his VAT quarter ended 31 July 20X7.

He has made 5 sales, each standard rated, for net amounts of £2,000, £3,600, £4,000, £6,000 and £10,000. In each case he allowed a cash discount of 5%.

He has made various purchases. He has a bundle of less detailed invoices totalling £1,880 in which VAT was included at the rate of 17.5%. In addition he has one invoice from a major supplier for £11,750 (including VAT).

He has paid wages of £6,000, and received insurance proceeds of £5,200 following fire damage.

Fill in boxes 1 to 9 on the VAT return for the three months to 31 July 20X7.

Value Added Tax Return
For the period
to

HM Customs and Excise

For Official Use

┌   ┐

└   ┘

Fold Here

Registration number

Period

You could be liable to a financial penalty if your completed return and all the VAT payable are not received by the due date.

Due date:

For official use D O R only	

Before you fill in this form please read the notes on the back and the VAT leaflet *"Filling in your VAT return"*. Fill all boxes clearly in ink, and write 'none' where necessary. Don't put a dash or leave any box blank. If there are no pence write "00" in the pence column. Do **not** enter more than one amount in any box.

£   p

For official use				£	p
	VAT due in this period on **sales** and other outputs	**1**			
	VAT due in this period on **acquisitions** from other **EC Member States**	**2**			
	Total VAT due (**the sum of boxes 1 and 2**)	**3**			
	VAT reclaimed in this period on **purchases** and other inputs (including acquisitions from the EC)	**4**			
	Net VAT to be paid to Customs or reclaimed by you (**Difference between boxes 3 and 4**)	**5**			
	Total value of **sales** and all other outputs excluding any VAT. **Include your box 8 figure**	**6**			00
	Total value of **purchases** and all other inputs excluding any VAT. **Include your box 9 figure**	**7**			00
	Total value of **all supplies** of goods and related services, excluding any VAT, to other **EC Member States**	**8**			00
	Total value of all **acquisitions** of goods and related services, excluding any VAT, from other **EC Member States**	**9**			00

If you are enclosing a payment please tick this box	DECLARATION: You, or someone on your behalf, must sign below.
	I, ... declare that the
	(Full name of signatory in BLOCK LETTERS)
	information given above is true and complete.
	Signature .... Date ....
	A false declaration can result in prosecution

SPECIAL CASES (VAT)

ACTIVITY 51

James has been using the cash accounting scheme for many years. All sales and purchases are made by cheque. He provides the following lists of invoices issued and received for the quarter ended 31 August 20X7:

(a)   Sales invoices

Date	Gross	VAT	Net	Paid
	£	£	£	
25.5.X7	1,645	245	1,400	3.6.X7
10.6.X7	1,175	175	1,000	21.6.X7
25.6.X7	2,350	350	2,000	11.7.X7
7.7.X7	1,880	280	1,600	23.8.X7
28.7.X7	2,115	315	1,800	3.9.X7
16.8.X7	2,585	385	2,200	29.8.X7
24.8.X7	1,410	210	1,200	15.9.X7

(b)   Purchase invoices

Date	Gross	VAT	Net	Paid
	£	£	£	
25.5.X7	705	105	600	29.6.X7
9.6.X7	940	140	800	29.6.X7
29.6.X7	1,175	175	1,000	30.7.X7
16.7.X7	3,525	525	3,000	30.7.X7
3.8.X7	705	105	600	29.8.X7
24.8.X7	470	70	400	28.9.X7

What are the details of outputs and output tax, and inputs and input tax to be entered on James' VAT return for the quarter to 31 August 20X7?

ACTIVITY 52

R Jones & Co Ltd made the following sales to Caroline:

Date	Type of supply	Gross
		£
1.1.X4	Standard rated	4,700
21.1.X4	Zero rated	5,000
12.2.X4	Standard rated	2,350
11.3.X4	Standard rated	3,525

On 24 April 20X4 Caroline paid £4,700 for invoice no 3083. A month later she was declared bankrupt, and R Jones & Co Ltd wrote off the remaining debt.

All the VAT had been accounted for on the return for the quarter ended 31 March 20X4. R Jones and Co Ltd allow debtors one calendar month for payment.

How much bad debt relief can be claimed and when?

ADMINISTRATION

ACTIVITY 53

Jack has been asked by one of his UK customers to send some goods to him through the post. Jack will make a separate charge for postage and packing. The goods themselves are zero rated. Should he charge VAT?

Use the VAT Guide to prepare your answer.

ACTIVITY 54

Robert and Richard Brooks have been trading in partnership, under the name R & R Services. They are registered for VAT, registration number 452 6870 01.

They decide to admit Naomi Fenn into partnership on 1 February 20X8, and to change the name to R 'N R Services

(a)   What is the time limit for notifying HM Customs and Excise? Use the VAT Guide to prepare your answer.

(b)   Draft a letter to HM Customs and Excise notifying them of the changes.

SPECIMEN SIMULATION

COVERAGE OF PERFORMANCE CRITERIA

The following performance criteria are covered in this simulation, in the tasks noted

Element	PC Coverage	Task(s)
7.1	**Prepare and present periodic performance reports**	
A	Consolidate information derived from different units of the organisation into the appropriate form.	1
B	Reconcile information derived from different information systems within the organisation.	1, 6
C	Compare results over time using an appropriate method that allows for changing price levels.	3
D	Account for transactions between separate units of the organisation in accordance with the organisation's procedures.	1
E	Calculate ratios and performance indicators in accordance with the organisation's procedures.	6
F	Prepare reports in the appropriate form and present them to management within the required timescales.	2, 5
7.2	**Prepare reports and returns for outside agencies**	
A	Identify, collate and present relevant information in accordance with the	4
B	Conventions and definitions used by outside agencies. Ensure calculations of ratios and performance indicators are accurate.	4
C	Obtain authorisation for the despatch of completed reports and returns from the appropriate person.	5
D	Presented reports and returns in accordance with outside agencies' requirements and deadlines.	4
7.3	**Prepare VAT returns**	
A	Complete and submit VAT returns correctly, using data from the appropriate recording systems, within the statutory time limits.	6
B	Correctly identify and calculate relevant inputs and outputs.	6
C	Ensure submissions are made in accordance with current legislation.	6, 8
D	Ensure guidance is sought from the VAT office when required, in a professional manner.	7

THE SITUATION

Your name is Amir Pindhi and you work as an Accounts Assistant for Homer Limited, Sestos Drive, Pantile Trading Estate CV32 1AW.

Homer Limited is a manufacturing company, producing a single product, the 'Bart'. The company's year end is 31 March.

Today's date is Monday 14 April 20X3.

DIVISIONAL STRUCTURE OF HOMER LIMITED

All production activities are carried out in the Manufacturing division. This division transfers most of its output to the Sales Division, which sells the output to external customers.

The Manufacturing Division transfers finished output to the Sales division at full production cost, but without any mark-up for profit. The Manufacturing division also sells some of its finished output direct to external customers.

ACCOUNTING FOR VAT

Homer Limited is registered for VAT.

Sales of Barts to UK customers are subject to VAT at the standard rate of 17.5%.

The company also exports to other countries within the European Union (EU). Such exports qualify as zero-rated. The company does not export to countries outside the EU. The company does not import any goods or services.

The local VAT office for Homer Limited is at Bell House, 33 Lambert Road, Coventry CV12 8TR.

APPLICATION FOR BANK LOAN

The company is about to seek a long-term loan from its bankers to finance expansion plans. The bank has requested some financial information in support of this application, and one of your responsibilities will be to present this information in the form required by the bank.

PRESENTING YOUR WORK

Unless you are told otherwise:

*   all ratios and statistics should be computed and presented to two decimal places;

*   monetary amounts should be computed and presented to the nearest penny.

THE TASKS TO BE COMPLETED

TASK 1   Refer to the table in Appendix 1 which analyses monthly sales achieved by each of the company's two divisions during the years ended 31 March 20X2 and 31 March 20X3.

- Consolidate these figures to arrive at the monthly sales and cumulative sales for each month in the two year period. Note that this task relates only to sales made to external customers, not to transfers within the company from the Manufacturing division to the Sales division. You should set out your answer on the schedule for Task 1 in the answer tables.

TASK 2   Using the figures calculated in Task 1, plot a line graph. The graph should show the cumulative sales achieved month by month during the year ended 31 March 20X2 and, as a separate line, the cumulative sales achieved month by month during the year ended 31 March 20X3. As in Task 1, you are concerned only with the sales to external customers, not with internal transfers from Manufacturing to Sales.

TASK 3   In Appendix 2 you will find month-by-month values of an index appropriate to the industry in which Homer operates. The values given are stated by reference to a base figure of 100.

- Calculate the indexed value of the monthly sales to external customers, in March 20X3 terms, for each month's sales in the year ended 31 March 20X3. Your answer should be set out in the answer table for Task 3 in accordance with the notes on that page.

TASK 4   Refer to the information in Appendix 3.

- Complete the loan application form on page 5 of the answer booklet.

- Write a memo to the Accountant, Sonia Liesl, enclosing the form for her attention and approval prior to its submission to the bank. Use the blank memo form on page 6 of the answer booklet and date your memo 14 April 20X3.

TASK 5   Write a memo to Sonia Liesl, presenting the following statistics for her information, and very briefly suggesting a possible reason for the movement in each statistic's value since year ended 31 March 20X2. (The 20X2 values are given in brackets below.)

- The gross profit percentage for year ended 31 March 20X3 (The percentage in year ended 31 March 20X2 was 43.15%).

- The net profit percentage for year ended 31 March 20X3 (20X2: 7.84%).

- The production cost per 'Bart' produced and sold in year ended 31 March 20X3 (20X2: £10.83).

- The value of sales earned per employee in year ended 31 March 20X3 (20X2: £26,018.13).

Date your memo 14 April 20X3.

TASK 6   Refer to the information in Appendix 4 that relates to the company's VAT return for the quarter ended on 31 March 20X3.

- Complete the blank return in the answer tables. Note that the return is to be signed by the Accountant, Sonia Liesl, and that payment of any balance due to Customs & Excise will be made by cheque.

TASK 7   Refer to the memo from Sonia Liesl in Appendix 5.

- Draft a letter to your local VAT office (in the name of Sonia Liesl) asking for the required information.

TASK 8   Reply to Sonia Liesl's memo giving her the brief details she requests, and enclosing the draft letter prepared in Task 7 above.

FOULKS LYNCH
PUBLICATIONS

APPENDIX 1

MONTHLY SALES DURING THE YEARS ENDED 31 MARCH 20X2 AND 31 MARCH 20X3

All figures in £000. All figures exclude VAT.

	Sales Division	Manufacturing Division		
	Total	*To external customers*	*To Sales Division*	*Total*
20X1/20X2				
April	350	34	185	219
May	225	46	128	174
June	190	32	96	128
July	255	54	138	192
August	310	36	166	202
September	238	24	148	172
October	220	20	125	145
November	295	34	172	206
December	240	39	182	221
January	257	20	150	170
February	230	14	155	169
March	340	45	218	263
20X2/20X3				
April	339	42	197	239
May	189	53	119	172
June	223	14	109	123
July	295	44	214	258
August	280	50	176	226
September	265	34	138	172
October	219	12	119	131
November	322	50	170	220
December	316	39	180	219
January	281	29	148	177
February	248	24	168	192
March	240	51	185	236

APPENDIX 2

Industrial index: base = 100

20X2	April	123.8
	May	124.4
	June	124.9
	July	125.7
	August	126.3
	September	127.0
	October	127.5
	November	128.1
	December	128.9
20X3	January	129.6
	February	130.2
	March	131.0

APPENDIX 3

Statistical information relating to year ended 31 March 20X3

Production cost of Barts produced and sold in the year	£2,190,000
Gross profit for the year	£1,470,000
Administration costs for the year	£580,000
Distribution costs for the year	£430,000
Total of all other costs for the year	£150,000
Net profit for the year before taxation	£310,000
Net profit for the previous year before taxation	£278,000
Total capital employed	£6,590,000
Number of Barts produced and sold in the year	199,000
Average number of employees in the year	143

APPENDIX 4

The following details have been extracted from the company's daybooks.

(All figures are exclusive of VAT.)

SALES DAY BOOK TOTALS

QUARTER ENDED 31 MARCH 20X3

	January	February	March	Total
	£	£	£	£
UK sales: standard rated	282,862.57	245,871.89	269,088.11	797,822.57
EU sales: zero-rated	27,143.05	26,126.66	21,920.34	75,190.05
Total	310,005.62	271,998.55	291,008.45	873,012.62
VAT on UK sales	49,500.95	43,027.58	47,090.42	139,618.95

PURCHASES DAY BOOK TOTALS

QUARTER ENDED 31 MARCH 20X3

	January	February	March	Total
	£	£	£	£
Purchases/expenses	186,007.66	163,265.69	171,295.45	520,568.80
VAT on purchases/expenses	32,551.34	28,571.50	29,976.70	91,099.54

A debt of £658, inclusive of VAT, was written off as bad in March 20X3.

The related sale was made in June 20X2. Bad debt relief is now to be claimed.

APPENDIX 5

<table>
<tr><td colspan="2" align="center">MEMO</td></tr>
<tr><td>To:</td><td>Amir Pindhi</td></tr>
<tr><td>From:</td><td>Sonia Liesl</td></tr>
<tr><td>Subject:</td><td>VAT on imports</td></tr>
<tr><td>Date:</td><td>11 April 20X3</td></tr>
</table>

As you may know, we have been in discussions with a supplier based in the Far East. We are considering importing certain components in future for use in our manufacturing activities.

Please could you remind me very briefly of the VAT implications if we decide to proceed with this. Please also draft a letter to the VAT office, in my name, requesting relevant publications so that we can be sure we account for the VAT correctly.

Thanks for your help.

ANSWER TABLES

TASK 1

Sales to external customers

Manufacturing and Sales divisions combined

	Monthly totals £'000	Cumulative total for the year £'000
20X1/20X2		
April		
May		
June		
July		
August		
September		
October		
November		
December		
January		
February		
March		
20X2/20X3		
April		
May		
June		
July		
August		
September		
October		
November		
December		
January		
February		
March		

TASK 3

Indexed sales to external customers

Manufacturing and Sales divisions combined

	Unadjusted totals £000	Index factor	Indexed totals £000
20X2/20X3			
April			
May			
June			
July			
August			
September			
October			
November			
December			
January			
February			
March			

Notes

1. In the first column, insert the monthly totals of external sales calculated in Task 1.

2. In the second column, insert the index factor required to convert to March 20X3 values.

3. In the third column, calculate the monthly sales in March 20X3 terms (to the nearest £1,000).

TASK 4

LOAN APPLICATION (extract)

Name of applicant company

Latest year for which accounting information is available

Total sales revenue

In latest year for which accounts are available £

In previous year £

Percentage change (+/-)

Net profit after all expenses, before taxation

In latest year for which accounts are available £

In previous year £

Percentage change (+/-)

Gross profit margin (%)

Net profit margin (%)

Return on capital employed (%)

Notes

1. In the case of a company with a divisional structure, all figures should refer to the results of the company as a whole, not to individual divisions within the company.

2. Unless otherwise stated, all questions relate to the latest year for which accounting information is available.

3. Figures should be actual historical values, with no indexing for inflation.

4. Return on capital employed is defined as net profit for the year before taxation, divided by total capital employed.

TASK 6

Value Added Tax Return
For the period
01-01-X3 **to** 31-03-X3

HM Customs and Excise

For Official Use

Registration number	Period
625 7816 29	03 X3

You could be liable to a financial penalty if your completed return and all the VAT payable are not received by the due date.

Due date: 30.04.X3

┌ ┐

HOMER LIMITED
SESTOS DRIVE
PANTILE TRADING ESTATE
CV32 1AW

└ ┘

For official use D O R only	

Fold Here

Before you fill in this form please read the notes on the back and the VAT leaflet *"Filling in your VAT return"*. Fill all boxes clearly in ink, and write 'none' where necessary. Don't put a dash or leave any box blank. If there are no pence write "00" in the pence column. Do **not** enter more than one amount in any box.

For official use			£	p
	VAT due in this period on **sales** and other outputs	**1**		
	VAT due in this period on **acquisitions** from other **EC Member States**	**2**		
	Total VAT due (**the sum of boxes 1 and 2**)	**3**		
	VAT reclaimed in this period on **purchases** and other inputs (including acquisitions from the EC)	**4**		
	Net VAT to be paid to Customs or reclaimed by you (**Difference between boxes 3 and 4**)	**5**		
	Total value of **sales** and all other outputs excluding any VAT. **Include your box 8 figure**	**6**		00
	Total value of **purchases** and all other inputs excluding any VAT. **Include your box 9 figure**	**7**		00
	Total value of **all supplies** of goods and related services, excluding any VAT, to other **EC Member States**	**8**		00
	Total value of all **acquisitions** of goods and related services, excluding any VAT, from other **EC Member States**	**9**		00

If you are enclosing a payment please tick this box	DECLARATION: You, or someone on your behalf, must sign below. I, ... declare that the (Full name of signatory in BLOCK LETTERS) information given above is true and complete. Signature .... Date .... **A false declaration can result in prosecution**

PRACTICE SIMULATION 1

COVERAGE OF PERFORMANCE CRITERIA

The following performance criteria are covered in this simulation, in the tasks noted

Element	PC Coverage	Task(s)
7.1	**Prepare and present periodic performance reports**	
A	Consolidate information derived from different units of the organisation into the appropriate form.	4
B	Reconcile information derived from different information systems within the organisation.	4
C	Compare results over time using an appropriate method that allows for changing price levels.	5
D	Account for transactions between separate units of the organisation in accordance with the organisation's procedures.	4
E	Calculate ratios and performance indicators in accordance with the organisation's procedures.	5
F	Prepare reports in the appropriate form and present them to management within the required timescales.	5
7.2	**Prepare reports and returns for outside agencies**	
A	Identify, collate and present relevant information in accordance with the	6
B	conventions and definitions used by outside agencies. Ensure calculations of ratios and performance indicators are accurate.	6
C	Obtain authorisation for the despatch of completed reports and returns from the appropriate person.	7
D	Presented reports and returns in accordance with outside agencies' requirements and deadlines.	6
7.3	**Prepare VAT returns**	
A	Complete and submit VAT returns correctly, using data from the appropriate recording systems, within the statutory time limits.	1, 2
B	Correctly identify and calculate relevant inputs and outputs.	2
C	Ensure submissions are made in accordance with current legislation.	2
D	Ensure guidance is sought from the VAT office when required, in a professional manner.	3

THE SITUATION

Your name is Sol Bellcamp and you work as an accounts assistant for a printing company, Hoddle Limited. Hoddle Limited is owned 100 per cent by another printing company, Kelly Limited. You report to the Group Accountant, Sherry Teddingham.

Hoddle Limited manufactures a wide range of printed materials such as cards, brochures and booklets. Most customers are based in the UK, but sales are also made to other countries in the European Union (EU). There are no exports to countries outside the EU. All of the company's purchases come from businesses within the UK.

Hoddle Limited is registered for VAT and it makes both standard-rated and zero-rated supplies to its UK customers. All sales to other EU countries qualify as zero-rated. The company's local VAT office is at Brendon House, 14 Abbey Street, Pexley PY2 3WR.

Kelly Limited is separately registered for VAT; there is no group registration in force. Both companies have an accounting year ending on 31 March. There are no other companies in the Kelly group.

Hoddle Limited is a relatively small company and sometimes suffers from shortage of capacity to complete customers' jobs. In these cases, the printing work is done by Kelly Limited. Kelly then sells the completed products to Hoddle for onward sale to the customer. The sale from Kelly to Hoddle is recorded in the books of each company at cost; Kelly does not charge a profit margin.

In this simulation you are concerned with the accounting year ended 31 March 20X2.

• To begin with you will be required to prepare the VAT return for Hoddle Limited in respect of the quarter ended 31 March 20X2.

• You will then be required to prepare certain reports, both for internal use and for an external interfirm comparison scheme, covering the whole accounting year ended 31 March 20X2. These reports will treat the two companies as a single group; they will contain consolidated figures, not figures for either of the two companies separately.

Today's date is 9 April 20X2.

THE TASKS TO BE COMPLETED

TASK 1   **Refer to the documents received from Hoddle Ltd's suppliers during** March 20X2 (Appendix 1). No entries have yet been made in Hoddle Ltd's books of account in respect of these documents. You are required to explain how you will treat each one of these documents when preparing Hoddle Ltd's VAT return for the period January to March 20X2.

TASK 2   Refer to the sales day book summary, purchases day book summary, cash book summary and petty cash book summary in Appendix 2. These have been printed out from Hoddle Ltd's computerised accounting system for the period January to March 20X2. (You are reminded that these summaries do not include the documents dealt with in task 1.) Refer also to the memo in Appendix 3. Using this information you are required to complete the VAT return of Hoddle Limited for the quarter ended 31 March 20X2. Your company will pay the VAT by cheque. A blank VAT return is provided.

TASK 3   The Group Accountant is considering adoption of the cash accounting scheme for VAT. He believes that Hoddle Limited (though not Kelly Limited) might qualify for the scheme. He has asked you to draft a letter to the VAT office, in his name, requesting certain details of the scheme. He is interested in the turnover limit for the scheme, particularly since Hoddle is a member of a group of companies, and in the effect of the scheme in dealing with bad debts. You are required to draft this letter.

TASK 4   Refer to the profit and loss account of Kelly Limited in Appendix 4, which covers the period 1 January to 31 March 20X2. You are required to prepare a profit and loss account for the same period in which the results of Hoddle and Kelly are consolidated. Enter your answer on the form provided, as follows:

- Enter the results of Kelly in the first column of the form.

- Using the information already provided for earlier tasks construct the results of Hoddle Ltd and enter them in the second column. Note that Hoddle Ltd's stock at 1 January 20X2 was valued at £14,638, while stock at 31 March 20X2 was valued at £16,052.

- Make appropriate adjustments in the third column to eliminate the effects of trading between Kelly and Hoddle.

- Calculate the consolidated figures and enter them in the fourth column.

TASK 5   Refer to the information in Appendix 5 and Appendix 6. Using this, and information already provided for earlier tasks, you are required to prepare a report for the Accountant on the group results for the year ended 31 March 20X2. Your report should contain the following:

- Key ratios: gross profit margin; net profit margin; return on shareholders' capital employed.

- Sales revenue for each quarter, both in actual terms and indexed to a common base.

- A pie chart showing the proportion of annual (unindexed) sales earned in each quarter.

Note that you are not required to comment on the results for the year, merely to present them according to the instructions above.

TASK 6   You are required to complete the interfirm comparison form.

TASK 7   You are required to prepare a memo to the Group Accountant enclosing the interfirm comparison form for authorisation before despatch. Use the blank page in the answer booklet.

APPENDIX 1

Engineering Supplies Limited

Haddlefield Road, Blaysley CG6 6AW
Tel/fax: 01376 44531

Hoddle Limited
22 Formguard Street
Pexley
PY6 3QW

SALES INVOICE NO: *2155*

Date: *27 March 20X2*

VAT omitted in error from invoice no 2139

	£
£2,667.30 @ 17.5%	466.77
Total due	466.77

Terms: net 30 days

VAT registration: 318 1827 58

ALPHA STATIONERY

Ainsdale Centre, Mexton EV1 4DF
Telephone 01392 43215

26-Mar 20X2

1 box transparent folders: red

Total incl VAT @ 17.5%	14.84
Amount tendered	20.00
Change	5.16

VAT registration: 356 7612 33

JAMIESON & CO

Jamieson House, Baines Road, Gresham GM7 2PQ
Telephone: 01677 35567   Fax: 01677 57640

PROFORMA SALES INVOICE

VAT registration: *412 7553 67*

Hoddle Limited
22 Formguard Street
Pexley
PY6 3QW

For professional services in connection with debt collection	£
Our fees	350.00
VAT	61.25
Total due	411.25

A VAT invoice will be submitted when the total due is paid in full.

APPENDIX 2

HODDLE LIMITED: SALES DAY BOOK SUMMARY
JANUARY TO MARCH 20X2

	January £	February £	March £	Total £
UK: Zero-rated	20,091.12	22,397.00	23,018.55	65,506.67
UK: Standard rated	15,682.30	12,914.03	15,632.98	44,229.31
Other EU	874.12	4,992.66	5,003.82	10,870.60
VAT	2,744.40	2,259.95	2,735.77	7,740.12
Total	39,391.94	42,563.64	46,391.12	128,346.70

HODDLE LIMITED: PURCHASES DAY BOOK SUMMARY

JANUARY TO MARCH 20X2

	January £	February £	March £	Total £
Purchases	14,532.11	20,914.33	15,461.77	50,908.21*
Distribution expenses	4,229.04	3,761.20	5,221.43	13,211.67
Admin expenses	5,123.08	2,871.45	3,681.62	11,676.15
Other expenses	1,231.00	1,154.99	997.65	3,383.64
VAT	4,027.97	4,543.22	4,119.34	12,690.53
Total	29,143.20	33,245.19	29,481.81	91,870.20

* This figure includes £18,271 of purchases from Kelly Limited.

HODDLE LIMITED: CASH BOOK SUMMARY

JANUARY TO MARCH 20X2

	January £	February £	March £	Total £
Payments				
To creditors	12,901.37	15,312.70	18,712.44	46,926.51
To petty cash	601.40	555.08	623.81	1,780.29
Wages/salaries	5,882.18	6,017.98	6,114.31	18,014.47
Total	19,384.95	21,885.76	25,450.56	66,721.27
Receipts				
VAT from Customs & Excise	2,998.01			2,998.01
From customers	29,312.44	34,216.08	36,108.77	99,637.29
Total	32,310.45	34,216.08	36,108.77	102,635.30
Surplus for month	12,925.50	12,330.32	10,658.21	
Balance b/f	-8,712.41	4,213.09	16,543.41	
Balance c/f	4,213.09	16,543.41	27,201.62	

HODDLE LIMITED: PETTY CASH BOOK SUMMARY
JANUARY TO MARCH 20X2

	January £	February £	March £	Total £
Payments				
Stationery	213.85	80.12	237.58	531.55
Travel	87.34	76.50	102.70	266.54
Office expenses	213.66	324.08	199.51	737.25
VAT	86.55	74.38	84.02	244.95
Total	601.40	555.08	623.81	1,780.29
Receipts				
from cash book	601.40	555.08	623.81	1,780.29
Surplus for month	0.00	0.00	0.00	
Balance b/f	200.00	200.00	200.00	
Balance c/f	200.00	200.00	200.00	

APPENDIX 3

MEMO

To: Sol Bellcamp
From: Sherry Teddingham
Date: 6 April 20X2
Subject: Bad debt - Batty Limited

As you probably know, we have had great difficulty in persuading the above customer to pay what he owes us. We invoiced him in July 20X2 for £420 plus VAT at the standard rate, but he has always disputed the debt and it looks as though we will never recover it. We wrote it off to the bad debt account in March of this year, so you should take this into account when preparing the VAT return for the quarter just ended.

APPENDIX 4

KELLY LIMITED
PROFIT AND LOSS ACCOUNT
FOR THE THREE MONTHS ENDED 31 MARCH 20X2

	£	£
Sales to external customers		275,601
Sales to Hoddle Limited at cost		20,167*
Total sales		295,768
Opening stock	28,341	
Purchases	136,095	
	164,436	
Closing stock	31,207	
Cost of sales		133,229
Gross profit		162,539
Wages and salaries	47,918	
Distribution expenses	28,341	
Administration expenses	30,189	
Stationery	2,541	
Travel	2,001	
Office expenses	3,908	
Interest payable	12,017	
Other expenses	11,765	
		138,680
Net profit for the period		23,859

*   This figure includes £1,896 in respect of a job completed on 31 March 20X2 but not delivered to Hoddle Limited until 1 April 20X2. It is not included in Hoddle Ltd's purchases for the period ended 31 March.

KELLY AND HODDLE
CONSOLIDATED BALANCE SHEET AT 31 MARCH 20X2

	£	£
Fixed assets at net book value		1,229,348
Current assets		
Stock	49,155	
Trade debtors	223,009	
VAT recoverable	13,451	
Cash at bank and in hand	40,088	
	325,703	
Current liabilities		
Trade creditors	136,531	
Other creditors	11,740	
	148,271	
Net current assets		177,432
Total assets less current liabilities		1,406,780
Long-term liability		
Loan repayable in 20X8		372,072
		1,034,708
Capital and reserves		
Called up share capital		234,167
Retained profits		800,541
		1,034,708

APPENDIX 5

QUARTERLY CONSOLIDATED PROFIT AND LOSS ACCOUNTS
FOR THE YEAR ENDED 31 MARCH 20X2

	1 Apr 20X1 30 Jun 20X1 £	1 Jul 20X1 30 Sep 20X1 £	1 Oct 20X1 31 Dec 20X1 £	1 Jan 20X2 31 Mar 20X2 £	1 Apr 20X1 31 Mar 20X2 £
Sales	325,719	275,230	306,321		
Cost of sales	134,861	109,421	121,358		
Gross profit	190,858	165,809	184,963		
Wages and salaries	63,314	61,167	64,412		
Distribution expenses	34,217	30,135	31,221		
Administration expenses	34,765	33,012	36,415		
Stationery	2,981	2,671	3,008		
Travel	1,975	1,876	2,413		
Office expenses	4,412	4,713	3,083		
Interest payable	12,913	12,714	12,432		
Other expenses	10,981	16,421	15,431		
	165,558	162,709	168,415		
Net profit for the period	25,300	3,100	16,548		

Note for candidates: you are advised to complete the above schedule by filling in the figures for the final quarter in the fourth column and totalling the figures for the year in the final column.

APPENDIX 6

MEMO

To: Sol Bellcamp

From: Sherry Teddingham

Subject: Adjusting for the effects of price rises

Date: 2 April 20X2

When presenting your quarterly reports on group results please include an item of information additional to that which you normally present. As well as noting sales revenue by quarter, please present quarterly sales revenue adjusted to take account of price rises.

I have identified a suitable index as follows.

First quarter 20X0/X1 (base period)	231.8
First quarter 20X1/X2	239.3
Second quarter 20X1/X2	241.5
Third quarter 20X1/X2	244.0
Fourth quarter 20X1/X2	241.8

I will keep you informed of future movements in this index.

TASK 2

Value Added Tax Return
For the period
to

HM Customs and Excise

For Official Use

Registration number   Period

You could be liable to a financial penalty if
your completed return and all the VAT
payable are not received by the due date.

Due date:

| For official use D O R only | |

Fold Here

Before you fill in this form please read the notes on the back and the VAT leaflet *"Filling in your VAT return"*. Fill all boxes clearly in ink, and write 'none' where necessary. Don't put a dash or leave any box blank. If there are no pence write "00" in the pence column. Do **not** enter more than one amount in any box.

		£	p
VAT due in this period on **sales** and other outputs	1		
VAT due in this period on **acquisitions** from other **EC Member States**	2		
Total VAT due (**the sum of boxes 1 and 2**)	3		
VAT reclaimed in this period on **purchases** and other inputs (including acquisitions from the EC)	4		
Net VAT to be paid to Customs or reclaimed by you (**Difference between boxes 3 and 4**)	5		
Total value of **sales** and all other outputs excluding any VAT. **Include your box 8 figure**	6		00
Total value of **purchases** and all other inputs excluding any VAT. **Include your box 9 figure**	7		00
Total value of **all supplies** of goods and related services, excluding any VAT, to other **EC Member States**	8		00
Total value of all **acquisitions** of goods and related services, excluding any VAT, from other **EC Member States**	9		00

If you are enclosing a payment please tick this box	DECLARATION: You, or someone on your behalf, must sign below.
	I, ... declare that the
(Full name of signatory in BLOCK LETTERS)
information given above is true and complete.

Signature .... Date ....
A false declaration can result in prosecution |

FOULKS LYNCH PUBLICATIONS

TASK 4

CONSOLIDATED PROFIT AND LOSS ACCOUNT
FOR THE THREE MONTHS ENDED 31 MARCH 20X2

	Kelly £	Hoddle £	Adjustments £	Consolidated £
Sales	——	——		——
Opening stock				
Purchases	——	——		——
Closing stock	——	——		——
Cost of sales	——	——		——
	——	——		——
Gross profit	——	——		——
Wages and salaries				
Distribution expenses				
Administration expenses				
Stationery				
Travel				
Office expenses				
Interest payable				
Other expenses				
	——	——		——
	——	——		——
	——	——		——
Net profit for the period	——	——		——

TASK 6

INTERFIRM COMPARISON DATA (extracts)

Name of company ....

Year ended ....

Data

	£	% of sales	Industry best	Industry average
Sales				
Gross profit			62.1%	57.3%
Net profit			10.4%	5.8%
Fixed assets				
Current assets				
Current liabilities				
Return on capital employed			10.3%	9.0%

IMPORTANT NOTE

BEFORE COMPLETING THIS FORM YOU SHOULD READ THE EXPLANATORY NOTES BELOW

COMPLETING THE IFC DATA FORM

Explanatory notes

Note 1

'Sales' means sales to external customers. Inter-company, inter-divisional or inter-branch sales should be excluded.

Note 2

Fixed assets should be stated at net book value.

Note 3

Return on capital employed is net profit before interest charges, divided by the total of fixed assets (stated at net book value) and net current assets.

PRACTICE SIMULATION 2

COVERAGE OF PERFORMANCE CRITERIA

The following performance criteria are covered in this simulation.

Element	PC Coverage	Task(s)
7.1	**Prepare and present periodic performance reports**	
A	Consolidate information derived from different units of the organisation into the appropriate form.	–
B	Reconcile information derived from different information systems within the organisation.	–
C	Compare results over time using an appropriate method that allows for changing price levels.	2
D	Account for transactions between separate units of the organisation in accordance with the organisation's procedures.	–
E	Calculate ratios and performance indicators in accordance with the organisation's procedures.	1
F	Prepare reports in the appropriate form and present them to management within the required timescales.	2, 3, 4, 5, 6, 7
7.2	**Prepare reports and returns for outside agencies**	
A	Identify, collate and present relevant information in accordance with the	8
B	conventions and definitions used by outside agencies. Ensure calculations of ratios and performance indicators are accurate.	8
C	Obtain authorisation for the despatch of completed reports and returns from the appropriate person.	9
D	Presented reports and returns in accordance with outside agencies' requirements and deadlines.	8
7.3	**Prepare VAT returns**	
A	Complete and submit VAT returns correctly, using data from the appropriate recording systems, within the statutory time limits.	–
B	Correctly identify and calculate relevant inputs and outputs.	–
C	Ensure submissions are made in accordance with current legislation.	–
D	Ensure guidance is sought from the VAT office when required, in a professional manner.	–

THE SITUATION

The profit and loss figures of Edwards Electronics Ltd for the past three years are as follows:

Financial year *(to 31 December annually)*	*20X0* £'000	*20X1* £'000	*20X2* £'000
Sales revenue	403.2	423.0	442.8
Cost of sales	(216.6)	(235.0)	(242.3)
Gross profit	186.6	188.0	200.5
Other income	4.4	8.2	16.8
	191.0	196.2	217.3
General expenses			
Administrative expense	(129.4)	(132.4)	(131.2)
Sales and distribution costs	(43.7)	(42.8)	(44.6)
Interest costs	(6.8)	(7.0)	(12.2)
Net profit	11.1	14.0	29.3
Taxation	(3.9)	(5.3)	(11.7)
Profit after taxation	7.2	8.7	17.6
Dividends	(3.8)	(4.5)	(8.8)
Retained profits	3.4	4.2	8.8

The company finance director, Jeff Thompson, has been analysing the results and has produced the following additional detail of factors that have affected the company position over the three year period:

Financial performance affectors – 20X0–20X2

	20X0	20X1	20X2
Inflation indices (prices basically rising by 6% per annum)	112.0	118.72	125.84
Average interest rate over the financial year (as borne by Edwards Electronics Ltd)	18%	19%	12.5%

Balance sheet figures (to 31 December annually)

Financial year	20X0 £'000	20X1 £'000	20X2 £'000
Fixed assets	180.2	189.7	197.6
Current assets			
Stocks	71.0	80.6	91.0
Debtors and prepayments	78.1	81.9	88.1
Bank and cash	42.0	37.2	32.0
Current liabilities			
Trade creditors	(96.2)	(80.8)	(63.2)
Other creditors and accruals	(22.2)	(18.1)	(19.8)
Bank loan (long-term)	(17.2)	(18.6)	(45.0)
Net total assets	235.7	271.9	280.7
Financed by			
Capital	188.0	220.0	220.0
Retained profits	47.7	51.9	60.7
	235.7	271.9	280.7

Further information

Stocks at beginning of 20X0 = £68,300

	20X0	20X1	20X2
Annual purchases	219.3	244.6	252.7

THE TASKS TO BE COMPLETED

TASK 1

You have been asked by Jeff Thompson to analyse company condition and performance – initially by evaluating the condition and performance ratios suggested in the following pro-forma company analysis sheets:

Liquidity/Cashflow indicators			
Financial year	*20X0*	*20X1*	*20X2*
Current ratio: [Current assets: Current liabilities]			
Acid test ratio: [Current assets – Stocks: Current liabilities]			
Cash ratio: [Cash: Current liabilities]			

Performance indicators			
Financial year	*20X0*	*20X1*	*20X2*
Return on capital employed (ROCE) [Net profit/shareholder's investment × 100 (%)]			
Net profit margin [Net profit/Sales × 100 (%)]			
Asset efficiency/Turnover [Sales/Net total assets]			
Gross profit margin [Gross profit/Sales × 100 (%)]			
Expense: Sales ratios Admin. expenses: Sales Distribution costs: Sales Interest costs: Sales [All measured as % figures]			
Fixed asset efficiency/Turnover [Sales/Fixed assets]			
Stock turnover [Cost of sales: Average stock]			
Debtor turnover [Sales: Debtors]			

Debtor payment period [Debtors/Sales × 365]			
Creditor turnover [Purchases: Creditors]			
Creditor payment period [Creditors/Purchases × 365]			

TASK 2

Jeff Thompson has asked you to confirm his views on company performance over the three-year period. Make your responses in short (but *clear* and *full*) note form and support with the figures you calculated for Task 1. Jeff's views are expressed in the following notes:

1. **The inflation indices given in my earlier note indicate an inflation rate of 6% annually over 20X1 and 20X2.**

   Comment

2. **The sales position is not healthy. Sales revenues have been growing and sales prices have been increasing roughly in line with inflation rates. However, inflation-adjusted 20X2 and 20X3 sales revenue figures to 20X1 price levels indicate that sales volumes have been falling.**

   Comment

3. **The improved company performance over the three year period is largely a product of highly-effective cost control as indicated by cost of sales: sales and expenses: sales ratios.**

   Comment

4.   The balance sheet figures show outstanding debt liabilities at the end of each year. These figures are not reflective/representative of the average amount of debt outstanding over the whole of each respective year.

Using the figures for the average interest rate charged to us annually and our annual interest charges in the profit and loss account (from the earlier statements), the average amounts of interest-bearing debt over each year have been £37,777, £36,842 and £97,600 respectively.

Comment

5.   The proportion of company profits taken up by taxation has increased over the three-year period.

Comment

6.   Overall total profits have improved over the three-year period and the shareholders have benefited from the improvement. The company is in a healthier state generally.

Comment

The following analysis of sales revenue figures over the period 20X0–20X2 has been provided by Jeff Thompson:

Financial year	20X0 £'000	20X1 £'000	20X2 £'000
Sales revenue Breakdown:	403.2	423.0	442.8
3 months to 31 March	78.8	84.6	91.0

FOULKS LYNCH
PUBLICATIONS

3 months to 30 June	107.2	116.4	119.6
3 months to 30 September	85.9	93.4	98.2
3 months to 31 December	131.3	128.6	134.0

TASK 3

Jeff has requested that you work time series analysis on the quarterly figures to present underlying trends as well as seasonal effects, quarter by quarter, over the three-year period. A pro-forma appears below:

TIME SERIES ANALYSIS				
				Figures in £'000
Time periods 20X0	Quarterly figures	4-quarterly moving average figures [Gen. trend]	4-quarterly moving average figures [Centred trend]	Seasonal effects [per quarter]
3 months to 31 March	78.8			
3 months to 30 June	107.2			
3 months to 30 September				
3 months to 31 December				
20X1				
3 months to 31 March				
3 months to 30 June				
3 months to 30 September				
3 months to 31 December				
20X2				
3 months to 31 March				
3 months to 30 June				
3 months to 30 September				
3 months to 31 December				

TASK 4

A chart is required for management. The chart should show a graph line for (actual) sales figures quarter by quarter and a graph line for the centred moving average trend. Prepare the necessary chart on the following pro-forma:

Time series chart – Sales revenues

Period of analysis – Financial years 20X0 – 20X2

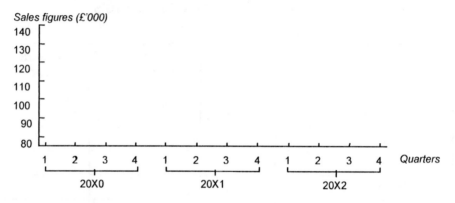

What is an average seasonal effect for a quarter ending on 30 September? Use your computations in task 4 to evaluate this.

TASK 5

The management of Edwards Electronics Ltd requires a bar chart presentation of the quarterly sales results over the 20X0–20X2 period. The request is that you prepare multiple bar charts. Four bars (one representing each quarter) should be shown side by side for each year to represent the results for that year. The charts are required on the pro-forma below:

Sales revenues – Quarterly results

Period of analysis – Financial years 20X0 – 20X2

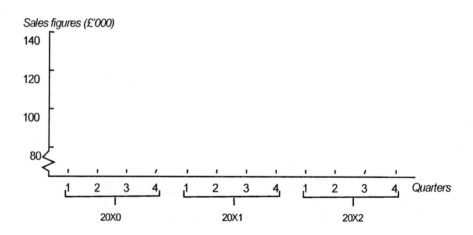

FOULKS LYNCH
PUBLICATIONS

TASK 6

The company also wants to display the sales results for 20X2 in the form of a pie chart; the pie chart should show the breakdown of total sales revenues for 20X2 into the proportions earned in each quarter. Prepare a suitable pie chart for the company:

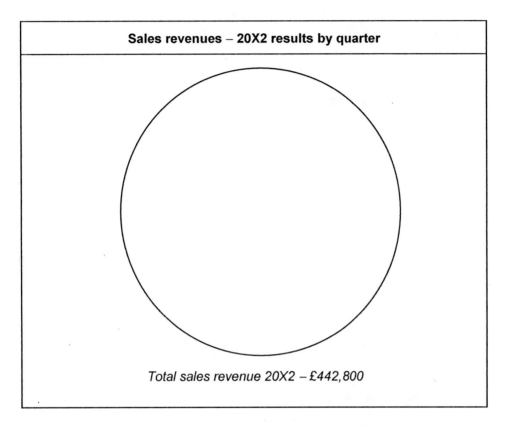

Sales revenues – 20X2 results by quarter

Total sales revenue 20X2 – £442,800

TASK 7

As part of the analysis for financial year 20X2, Jeff Thompson has asked you to analyse results for production and sales of the Tristar TV, a relatively new company product. Computer printouts of results for the product over 20X2 are as follows:

Actual sales:	190
Actual revenue:	£46,550
Actual production:	205
Actual machine hours:	102.5 hours
Actual assembly time:	369 hours

The analysis is to be made using the company pro-forma analysis sheets which follow. Complete the analysis sheets appropriately, to two decimal places.

Edwards Electronics Ltd
Production evaluation

Product:

Period:

Production per assembly hour:

Production per machine hour:

Revenue per unit

TASK 8

Jeff Thompson has requested that you complete a return required by the Association of Electrical Contractors in respect of the financial year ending 31 December 20X2:

A
E
C
Association of Electrical Contractors
18, Grafton Way, Herts, HA3 4PF

Annual performance results

ROCE
[% on owner's investment] ☐   Debtor period ☐

Gross margin on sales ☐

Creditor period ☐

Net margin on sales ☐
[using net profit before tax]
Asset turnover ☐   Stock period ☐
[Sales/Net total assets]

[All periods in days]

Above figures taken from financial statements for the year to/as at . . . .

Results will be confidentially held and used only to produce general descriptive statistical information for the use of the Association and its members.

TASK 9

Draft a memo to Jeff Thompson asking him to authorise the return for the Association of Electrical Contractors prior to its despatch.

PRACTICE SIMULATION 3

COVERAGE OF PERFORMANCE CRITERIA

The following performance criteria are covered in this simulation, in the tasks noted

Element	PC Coverage	Task(s)
7.1	**Prepare and present periodic performance reports**	
A	Consolidate information derived from different units of the organisation into the appropriate form.	–
B	Reconcile information derived from different information systems within the organisation.	–
C	Compare results over time using an appropriate method that allows for changing price levels.	1, 3
D	Account for transactions between separate units of the organisation in accordance with the organisation's procedures.	–
E	Calculate ratios and performance indicators in accordance with the organisation's procedures.	4
F	Prepare reports in the appropriate form and present them to management within the required timescales.	2, 5
7.2	**Prepare reports and returns for outside agencies**	
A	Identify, collate and present relevant information in accordance with the	–
B	conventions and definitions used by outside agencies. Ensure calculations of ratios and performance indicators are accurate.	–
C	Obtain authorisation for the despatch of completed reports and returns from the appropriate person.	–
D	Presented reports and returns in accordance with outside agencies' requirements and deadlines.	–
7.3	**Prepare VAT returns**	
A	Complete and submit VAT returns correctly, using data from the appropriate recording systems, within the statutory time limits.	–
B	Correctly identify and calculate relevant inputs and outputs.	–
C	Ensure submissions are made in accordance with current legislation.	–
D	Ensure guidance is sought from the VAT office when required, in a professional manner.	–

THE SITUATION

Mills Carpets Ltd specialises in the production of woven wool Axminster and Wilton carpets.

Analysis of sales and prices for the last five years, together with the general index of retail prices (IRP) over the same period is given below.

Carpet production 20X1 to 20X5

	Year				
	20X1	*20X2*	*20X3*	*20X4*	*20X5*
Sales/Production ('000 sq yards)					
Axminster	10.2	10.8	11.3	11.8	12.3
Wilton	32.7	36.2	39.1	43.5	47.2
Selling price (£ per sq yard)					
Axminster	9.3	9.8	10.4	10.8	11.1
Wilton	12.3	13.1	13.8	14.9	15.6
IRP (base year = 100)	201	211	222	230	237

(Year 20X5 is the last full accounting year)

THE TASKS TO BE COMPLETED

TASK 1

Calculate the total value of annual sales each year. Use the IRP to deflate these values to give the 'real terms' sales values at year 20X1 prices.

(Value = Price × Quantity)

$$\text{Deflated value at 20X1 prices} = \frac{\text{Actual value} \times \text{IRP for 20X1}}{\text{IRP for current year}}$$

	20X1	*20X2*	*20X3*	*20X4*	*20X5*
Sales value of Axminster (£'000)					
Sales value of Wilton (£'000)					
Total sales value (£'000)					
Value at 20X1 prices (£'000)					

FOULKS LYNCH
PUBLICATIONS

TASK 2

Plot graphs of sales volume per year of each type of carpet on the same axes with time on the horizontal axis. Use these to obtain extrapolated forecasts of production of each type of carpet for 20X6.

Sales/Production
('000 sq yards)

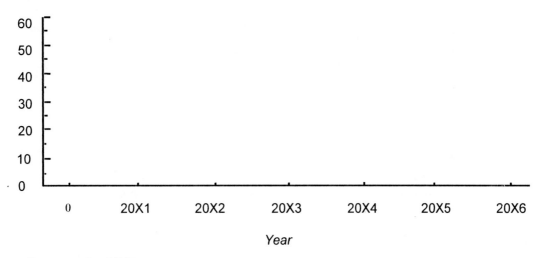

Year

Forecasts for 20X6
Axminister production:
Wilton production:

TASK 3

The following price indices are available which are appropriate for the carpet industry:

	20X1	*20X2*	*20X3*	*20X4*	*20X5*
Axminster	100	105	112	116	119
Wilton	100	107	112	121	127
IRP (20X1 = 100)	100	105.0	110.4	114.4	117.9

Write a memo to the sales director analysing sales and price variations and trends over the period 20X1 to 20X5 and give a statistical forecast of sales volume for 20X6.

TASK 4

Franklin plc is a competitor in the same industry and it has been operating for many years. You have obtained the following information relating to Franklin plc:

(a) **Summarised profit and loss accounts for the years ended 31 December**

	20X2		20X3		20X4	
	£'000	£'000	£'000	£'000	£'000	£'000
Turnover		3,120		2,700		3,000
Materials	630		480		600	
Labour	480		480		600	
Overhead	390		420		450	
		(1,500)		(1,380)		(1,650)
Gross profit		1,620		1,320		1,350
Administrative expenses	780		690		720	
Distribution costs	750		570		690	
		(1,530)		(1,260)		(1,410)
Profit on ordinary activities before taxation		90		60		(60)

(b) **Extracts from balance sheet at 31 December**

	20X2		20X3		20X4	
	£'000	£'000	£'000	£'000	£'000	£'000
Fixed assets at net book value		1,170		1,110		1,050
Raw materials	300		300		300	
Work in progress and finished goods	480		450		480	
Debtors	390		420		450	
		1,170		1,170		1,230
		2,340		2,280		2,280
Creditors: Amounts falling due within one year (including bank overdraft)		(810)		(810)		(870)
Capital employed		1,530		1,470		1,410

FOULKS LYNCH
PUBLICATIONS

(c)   No fixed assets were purchased or sold by Franklin plc between 20X2 and 20X4.

Complete the table below:

	20X2	20X3	20X4
Percentage to turnover:			
Gross profit			
Net profit			
Materials			
Labour			
Overhead			
Administration			
Distribution			
Percentage change in sales over previous year			
ROCE $\dfrac{\text{Profit before tax}}{\text{Total assets less current liabilities at year end}} \times 100$			
$\dfrac{\text{Turnover}}{\text{Fixed assets}}$			
Current ratio			
Quick ratio			
Stock turnover $\dfrac{\text{Cost of sales}}{\text{Year-end stock}}$			
Raw material stock turnover $\dfrac{\text{Cost of materials}}{\text{Year-end materials stock}}$			
Debtor collection period			

TASK 7

Prepare a report to the board of directors of Mills Carpets Ltd analysing the profitability and liquidity of Franklin plc. Also include a section on the limitations of the data upon which you have prepared your analysis

FOULKS LYNCH
PUBLICATIONS

PRACTICE SIMULATION 4

COVERAGE OF PERFORMANCE CRITERIA

The following performance criteria are covered in this simulation, in the tasks noted

Element	PC Coverage	Task(s)
7.1	**Prepare and present periodic performance reports**	
A	Consolidate information derived from different units of the organisation into the appropriate form.	–
B	Reconcile information derived from different information systems within the organisation.	–
C	Compare results over time using an appropriate method that allows for changing price levels.	–
D	Account for transactions between separate units of the organisation in accordance with the organisation's procedures.	–
E	Calculate ratios and performance indicators in accordance with the organisation's procedures.	1
F	Prepare reports in the appropriate form and present them to management within the required timescales.	–
7.2	**Prepare reports and returns for outside agencies**	
A	Identify, collate and present relevant information in accordance with the	–
B	conventions and definitions used by outside agencies. Ensure calculations of ratios and performance indicators are accurate.	–
C	Obtain authorisation for the despatch of completed reports and returns from the appropriate person.	–
D	Presented reports and returns in accordance with outside agencies' requirements and deadlines.	–
7.3	**Prepare VAT returns**	
A	Complete and submit VAT returns correctly, using data from the appropriate recording systems, within the statutory time limits.	2
B	Correctly identify and calculate relevant inputs and outputs.	1, 2
C	Ensure submissions are made in accordance with current legislation.	2
D	Ensure guidance is sought from the VAT office when required, in a professional manner.	3, 4

THE SITUATION

You work part-time as the bookkeeper and accounts clerk for a firm that supplies and fits kitchens in the south west London area. The business is known as Simons Kitchens. One of your duties is to complete the quarterly VAT return for the period to 31 October 20X7.

The system that the business adopts is that when an order is placed for a kitchen then a deposit of £80 plus VAT at 17.5% is payable immediately. The remaining amount due is usually invoiced on the date of completion of the kitchen unless agreed otherwise with the client.

THE TASKS TO BE COMPLETED

TASK 1

The sales invoices and purchase invoices for the period have been passed on to you together with a memorandum from the owner of the business, Jean Simons, regarding various other aspects that she thinks will be relevant. These invoices and memorandum are in the Appendices 1, 2 and 3 of this assessment. You are required to fill in the figures that would appear in boxes 1 to 9 on the VAT return from the information provided and write up the VAT account.

VAT account

£	£

VAT Return

**Value Added Tax Return
For the period
to**

HM Customs and Excise

For Official Use

Registration number

Period

You could be liable to a financial penalty if your completed return and all the VAT payable are not received by the due date.

Due date:

| For official use D O R only | |

Fold | Here

Before you fill in this form please read the notes on the back and the VAT leaflet *"Filling in your VAT return"*. Fill all boxes clearly in ink, and write 'none' where necessary. Don't put a dash or leave any box blank. If there are no pence write "00" in the pence column. Do **not** enter more than one amount in any box.

For official use			£	p
	VAT due in this period on **sales** and other outputs	**1**		
	VAT due in this period on **acquisitions** from other **EC Member States**	**2**		
	Total VAT due (**the sum of boxes 1 and 2**)	**3**		
	VAT reclaimed in this period on **purchases** and other inputs (including acquisitions from the EC)	**4**		
	Net VAT to be paid to Customs or reclaimed by you (**Difference between boxes 3 and 4**)	**5**		
	Total value of **sales** and all other outputs excluding any VAT. **Include your box 8 figure**	**6**		00
	Total value of **purchases** and all other inputs excluding any VAT. **Include your box 9 figure**	**7**		00
	Total value of **all supplies** of goods and related services, excluding any VAT, to other **EC Member States**	**8**		00
	Total value of all **acquisitions** of goods and related services, excluding any VAT, from other **EC Member States**	**9**		00

If you are enclosing a payment please tick this box	DECLARATION: You, or someone on your behalf, must sign below.
	I, ... declare that the (Full name of signatory in BLOCK LETTERS) information given above is true and complete. Signature .... Date .... **A false declaration can result in prosecution**

TASK 2

Next week the business is due a control visit by a Customs and Excise officer. Jean has asked you to put in writing for her the purpose of such visits and any action that the officer might take if he disagrees with any tax returns that have been made.

MEMORANDUM

TO:

FROM:

DATE:

SUBJECT:

TASK 3

Jean also has some further queries about VAT and VAT documentation that she would like clarified before the control visit. Write a memorandum to her on each of the following items.

(1)   What are exempt and zero rated supplies?

(2)   If any of my supplies are exempt or zero rated then how will this affect the calculation of VAT payable?

(3)   I sometimes receive credit notes from suppliers for goods that I have returned. If the credit note is to serve as valid documentation for a reduction of VAT on purchases what information must it contain?

(4)   I sometimes buy goods for the business from my local hardware shop and I have noticed that the invoice only includes the total value of the goods and does not show the VAT separately. Is this valid for VAT purposes and if not what should I do about it?

(Your memorandum should be in proper memorandum format.)

APPENDIX 1 – SALES INVOICES

SALES INVOICE

Simons Kitchens
199 Waterhill Road
London
SW6 8IC

Tel: 0207 492 8833

VAT reg no: 832 2056 66

Invoice number: 5535

Date: 22 August 20X7

To: Mr G R Wilson
               73A Baldwin Rise
               London
               SW4

Deposit of £94 including VAT at 17.5%

SALES INVOICE

SIMONS KITCHENS
199 Waterhill Road
London
SW6 8IC

Tel: 0207 492 8833

VAT reg no: 832 2056 66

Date: 22 August 20X7

Invoice number: 5536

To: Mrs J Jepson
               28 Margrave Hill
               London
               SW11

	VAT rate	£
Work performed:		
To supply and fit white lacquered kitchen code LDW 57	17.5%	6,660.00
Less: Deposit paid 1 July 20X7	17.5%	80.00
Total excluding VAT		6,580.00
VAT at 17.5%		1,151.50
Total including VAT		7,731.50

Terms: Strictly payable within 30 days.

SALES INVOICE

SIMONS KITCHENS
199 Waterhill Road
London
SW6 8IC

Tel:	0207 492 8833
VAT reg no:	832 2056 66
Date:	12 September 20X7
Invoice number:	5537
To:	Mr G R Wilson 73A Baldwin Rise London SW4

	VAT rate	£
Work performed: Supply and fitting of dark oak kitchen units code DO 81	17.5%	2,900.00
Less: Deposit paid on 15 July	17.5%	80.00
Total excluding VAT		2,820.00
VAT at 17.5%		493.50
Total including VAT		3,313.50

Terms: Strictly payable within 30 days.

SALES INVOICE

SIMONS KITCHENS
199 Waterhill Road
London
SW6 8IC

Tel:	0207 492 8833
VAT reg no:	832 2056 66
Date:	12 September 20X7
Invoice number:	5537
To:	Mr G R Wilson 73A Baldwin Rise London SW4

	VAT rate	£
Work performed: Supply and fitting dark oak kitchen units code DO 81	17.5%	2,900.00
Less: Deposit paid 15 July	17.5%	80.00
Total excluding VAT		2,820.00
VAT at 17.5%		493.50
Total including VAT		3,313.50

Terms: Strictly payable within 30 days.

FOULKS LYNCH
PUBLICATIONS

SALES INVOICE

SIMONS KITCHENS
199 Waterhill Road
London
SW6 8IC

Tel: 0207 492 8833

VAT reg no: 832 2056 66

Date: 30 September 20X7

Invoice number: 5538

To: Mr F Clancy
                       21 Edale Drive
                       London
                       SW18

	VAT rate	£
Work performed:		
Supply and fitting limed oak kitchen units and AEG appliances	17.5%	9,375.62
Less: Deposit paid 14 July 20X7	17.5%	80.00
Total excluding VAT		9,295.62
VAT at 17.5%		1,626.74
Total including VAT		10,922.36

Terms: Strictly payable within 30 days.

SALES INVOICE

SIMONS KITCHENS
199 Waterhill Road
London
SW6 8IC

Tel: 0207 492 8833

VAT reg no: 832 2056 66

Date: 2 November 20X7

Invoice number: 5540

To: Mr S Singh
                       28 High Street
                       London
                       SW8

	VAT rate	£
Work performed:		
Supply and fitting medium dark oak kitchen units (code MO 54) and Hotpoint appliances completed on 28 October 20X7	17.5%	7,254.50
Total excluding VAT		7,254.50
VAT at 17.5%		1,269.54
Total including VAT		8,524.04

Terms: Strictly payable within 30 days.

APPENDIX 2 – PURCHASE INVOICES

MAGNUM KITCHENS
Tower Estate
London
SW6

VAT reg no: 892 6845 60

Date/tax point: 8 August 20X7

Invoice number: SK 52

To: Simons Kitchens
    199 Waterhill Road
    London
    SW6 8IC

	VAT rate	£
Supply of:		
13 kitchen units medium oak	17.5%	2,100.00
17 kitchen units dark oak	17.5%	2,800.00
Total excluding VAT		4,900.00
VAT @ 17.5%		857.50
Total including VAT		5,757.50

Terms: Payable within 60 days.

Expense claim form - Jean Simons

	Net	VAT	Gross
Client entertaining			
(bill attached)	117.00	20.48	137.48

FOULKS LYNCH
PUBLICATIONS

BROKEN HEART RESTAURANT
Middle Court
London
EC4

Date: 4 October 20X7

	£
3 × standard set lunch	96.00
Wine	21.00
	117.00
VAT at 17.5%	20.48
	137.48

Service is included.

ELLSE ELECTRICALS
9, Summer Way
London
SW19

VAT reg no: 834 3745 77

Invoice number: 92785

Date: 24 August 20X7

To: Simons Kitchens
                   199 Waterhill Road
                   London
                   SW6 8IC

	VAT rate	£
Supply of:		
AEG fridge/freezer	17.5%	359.00
Hotpoint washing machine	17.5%	269.00
Hotpoint tumble dryer	17.5%	199.00
Total excluding VAT		827.00
VAT @ 17.5%		141.83
Total including VAT		968.83

Terms: 2%/30 days
       net 60 days

ELLSE ELECTRICALS
9, Summer Way
London
SW19

VAT reg no: 834 3745 77

Invoice number: 92941

Date: 19 September 20X7

To: Simons Kitchens
          199 Waterhill Road
          London
          SW6 8IC

TAX CERTIFICATE

No payment is necessary for these goods. Output tax has been accounted for on the supply.

	VAT rate	£
Supply of:		
10 samples of halogen downlighter bulbs (cost price £7.48 each excluding VAT) (9 charged, one free)	17.5%	67.32
Total excluding VAT		67.32
VAT		11.78
Total including VAT		79.10

Terms: 2%/30 days
          net 60 days

NICHOLAS BAINS & CO
Fairacre Trading Estate
London
SW14

VAT reg no: 032 5485 68

Date: 1 October 20X7

To: Simons Kitchens
       199 Waterhill Road
       London
       SW6 8IC

	VAT rate	£
Supply of 11 units hand made - oak	17.5	3,100.00
Supply of 1 oak kitchen table	17.5	800.00
Total excluding VAT		3,900.00
VAT at 17.5%		682.50
Total including VAT		4,582.50

Terms: payable within 30 days

APPENDIX 3

MEMORANDUM TO BOOKKEEPER FROM JEAN SIMONS

MEMORANDUM

TO: Bookkeeper

FROM: Jean Simons

DATE: 4 November 20X7

SUBJECT: **VAT return**

Thank you for your note of 16 August 20X7 explaining the errors that you believed were made in the previous VAT return. Having checked the figures I can confirm that the tax payable was understated by £2,700 and the tax allowable was understated by £2,500. Please take whatever action is necessary to deal with this.

I am not sure whether or not the write off of bad debts is relevant to the VAT return but I know that you will need to know about them for writing up the accounts. In the last three months I have had to admit that there are two debts that I am sure will never be paid. One was an amount of £3,287.65 (including VAT) from Mr James Smith who was invoiced on 27 June 20X7 (invoice number 5503). The other was £1,957.55 (including VAT) from Mrs P Taylor-Young invoiced on 3 January 20X7 (invoice number 5479).

PRACTICE SIMULATION 5

COVERAGE OF PERFORMANCE CRITERIA

The following performance criteria are covered in this simulation, in the tasks noted

Element	PC Coverage	Task(s)
7.1	**Prepare and present periodic performance reports**	
A	Consolidate information derived from different units of the organisation into the appropriate form.	1
B	Reconcile information derived from different information systems within the organisation.	1, 6
C	Compare results over time using an appropriate method that allows for changing price levels.	3
D	Account for transactions between separate units of the organisation in accordance with the organisation's procedures.	1
E	Calculate ratios and performance indicators in accordance with the organisation's procedures.	5
F	Prepare reports in the appropriate form and present them to management within the required timescales.	2, 5
7.2	**Prepare reports and returns for outside agencies**	
A	Identify, collate and present relevant information in accordance with the	4
B	Conventions and definitions used by outside agencies. Ensure calculations of ratios and performance indicators are accurate.	4
C	Obtain authorisation for the despatch of completed reports and returns from the appropriate person.	5
D	Presented reports and returns in accordance with outside agencies' requirements and deadlines.	4
7.3	**Prepare VAT returns**	
A	Complete and submit VAT returns correctly, using data from the appropriate recording systems, within the statutory time limits.	6
B	Correctly identify and calculate relevant inputs and outputs.	6
C	Ensure submissions are made in accordance with current legislation.	6, 8
D	Ensure guidance is sought from the VAT office when required, in a professional manner.	7

THE SITUATION

Your name is Vinny Taswell and you work as an accounts assistant for Jacob Limited, Unit 7 Thamesview Business Park, Cultham CM5 8RW.

Jacob Limited is a manufacturing company, producing a single product, the 'Benji'. The company's year end is 31 December.

Today's date is Monday 15 January 20X5.

DIVISIONAL STRUCTURE OF JACOB LIMITED

The company is organised in two divisions: Manufacturing and Sales.

When goods are completed they are transferred from Manufacturing to Sales at full production cost (but without any profit mark-up).

The Sales division is then responsible for onward sale to external customers.

A few sales to external customers are also made by the Manufacturing division directly (i.e. without going through Sales).

ACCOUNTING FOR VAT

Jacob Limited is registered for VAT.

Sales of Benjis to UK customers are subject to VAT at the standard rate of 17.5%.

The company also exports to other countries within the European Union (EU). These exports qualify as zero-rated.

The company does not export to countries outside the EU.

The local VAT office for Jacob Limited is at 29 Parson Street, Cultham CM1 6TY.

THE MANUFACTURERS AND PRODUCERS ASSOCIATION

Jacob Limited is a member (membership number 225671) of a regional trades association, the Manufacturers and Producers Association.

The Association publishes statistics compiled from returns submitted by members each year.

One of your responsibilities is to complete the annual return for approval by your boss, the accountant Dan Asher, before submission to the Association.

THE TASKS TO BE COMPLETED

TASK 1   **In Appendix 1 there is a table which analyses monthly sales achieved by each** of the company's two divisions during 20X3 and 20X4.

Consolidate these figures to arrive at the monthly sales and cumulative sales for each month in the two year period. Note that this task relates only to sales made to external customers, not to transfers within the company from the Manufacturing division to the Sales division. You should set out your answer on the schedule provided in the answer tables below.

TASK 2   Using the figures calculated in Task 1, plot a line graph. The graph should show the cumulative sales achieved month by month during 20X3 and, as a separate line, the cumulative sales achieved month by month during the year 20X4. As in Task 1, you are concerned only with the sales to external customers, not with internal transfers from Manufacturing to Sales.

TASK 3   In Appendix 2 you will find month-by-month values of an index appropriate to the industry in which Jacob operates. The values given are stated by reference to a base figure of 100, which was the value of the index in the base period January 20X0.

Calculate the indexed value of the monthly sales to external customers, in January 20X0 terms, for each month's sales in the year 20X4. Your answer should be set out in the answer table provided for Task 3 and in accordance with the notes provided.

TASK 4   In Appendix 3 you will find certain statistical information relating to Jacob Limited during the year 20X4. Using this information, complete the company's annual return to the Manufacturers and Producers Association for the year 20X4. A blank return is provided in the answer tables below.

TASK 5   Write a memo to the accountant, Dan Asher, presenting the following statistics for his information, and very briefly suggesting a possible reason for the movement in each statistic's value since 20X3. (The 20X3 values are given in brackets below.)

- The gross profit percentage for 20X4 (The percentage in 20X3 was 44.10%).

- The net profit percentage for 20X4 (20X3: 8.01%).

- The production cost per 'Benji' produced and sold in 20X4 (20X3: £14.50).

- The value of sales earned per employee in 20X4 (20X3: £32,946.25).

Date your memo 14 April 20X3.

TASK 6   Refer to the information in Appendix 4 which relates to the company's VAT return for the quarter ended on 31 December 20X4. Complete the blank return provided in the answer tables. Note that the return is to be signed by the Accountant, Dan Asher, and that payment of any balance due to Customs & Excise will be made by cheque.

TASK 7   Refer to the memo from Dan Asher in Appendix 5. Draft a letter to your local VAT office (in the name of Dan Asher) asking whether the proposed new business activity would be classed as an exempt supply, and requesting printed information that will help you to deal with this matter appropriately.

TASK 8   Reply to Dan Asher's memo giving him the brief details he requests, and enclosing the draft letter prepared in Task 7 above.

APPENDIX 1

MONTHLY SALES DURING 20X3 AND 20X4

All figures in £000. All figures exclude VAT.

	Sales Division	Manufacturing Division		
	Total	To external customers	To Sales Division	Total
20X3				
January	410	42	220	262
February	265	52	154	206
March	228	36	110	146
April	299	66	161	227
May	368	45	200	245
June	280	30	171	201
July	262	22	145	167
August	345	40	201	241
September	281	45	216	261
October	300	25	180	205
November	269	17	180	197
December	398	56	253	309
20X4				
January	397	51	230	281
February	221	60	140	200
March	265	18	131	149
April	350	54	250	304
May	328	60	209	269
June	311	41	161	202
July	260	13	139	152
August	376	57	203	260
September	370	48	213	261
October	329	36	176	212
November	295	30	200	230
December	281	60	219	279

FOULKS LYNCH
PUBLICATIONS

APPENDIX 2

Industrial index: base = 100 (January 20X0)

20X4		
	January	111.6
	February	112.2
	March	113.0
	April	113.8
	May	114.4
	June	114.9
	July	115.7
	August	116.3
	September	117.0
	October	117.5
	November	118.1
	December	118.9

APPENDIX 3

Statistical information relating to year ended 31 December 20X4

Production cost of Benjis produced and sold in the year	£2,580,000
Gross profit for the year	£1,731,000
Administration costs for the year	£675,000
Distribution costs for the year	£511,000
Total of all other costs for the year	£176,000
Net profit for the year before taxation	£369,000
Net profit for the previous year before taxation	£278,000
Total capital employed	£7,748,000
Number of Benjis produced and sold in the year	168,000
Average number of employees in the year	134

APPENDIX 4

The following details have been extracted from the company's daybooks.

(All figures exclude VAT.)

SALES DAY BOOK TOTALS

QUARTER ENDED 31 DECEMBER 20X4

	October	November	December	Total
	£	£	£	£
UK sales: standard rated	334,131.90	290,436.56	317,860.74	942,429.20
EU sales: zero-rated	30,876.22	34,561.08	23,142.61	88,579.91
Total	365,008.12	324,997.64	341,003.35	1,031,009.11
VAT on UK sales	58,473.08	50,826.39	55,625.62	164,925.09

PURCHASES DAY BOOK TOTALS

QUARTER ENDED 31 DECEMBER 20X4

	October	November	December	Total
	£	£	£	£
Purchases/expenses	218,751.45	192,006.11	210,448.90	612,206.46
VAT on purchases/expenses	36,254.22	31,598.31	32,491.00	100,343.53

A debt of £705, including VAT, was written off as bad in December 20X4.

The related sale was made in March 20X4. Bad debt relief is now to be claimed.

MEMO

To:	Vinny Taswell
From:	Dan Asher
Date:	15 January 20X5
Subject:	VAT – exempt supplies

We are considering a small extension of our business activities by offering customers a product warranty on sales of our Benji. For a small extra charge, we would provide maintenance and support if customers had any difficulties with the product.

Although I'm not certain about this, I think that product warranties might be classed as an exempt supply for VAT purposes. Could you please write to our local VAT office for clarification, and ask them for any publications they may have that might be relevant? If I am correct, could you remind me (very briefly please) of the effect this would have on our ability to reclaim input VAT. The new activity would form only a tiny part of our overall business operations.

Thanks for your help.

FOULKS LYNCH
PUBLICATIONS

ANSWER TABLES

TASK 1

Sales to external customers

Manufacturing and Sales Divisions combined

	Monthly totals £000	Cumulative total for the year £000
20X3		
January		
February		
March		
April		
May		
June		
July		
August		
September		
October		
November		
December		
20X4		
January		
February		
March		
April		
May		
June		
July		
August		
September		
October		
November		
December		

Notes

1. In the first column, enter the monthly total of external sales achieved by the two divisions combined.

2. In the second column, enter the cumulative total of external sales in the accounting year.

TASK 3

Indexed sales to external customers

Manufacturing and Sales Divisions combined

	Unadjusted totals £000	Index factor	Indexed totals £000
20X4			
January			
February			
March			
April			
May			
June			
July			
August			
September			
October			
November			
December			

Notes

1.   In the first column, insert the monthly totals of external sales calculated in Task 1.

2.   In the second column, insert the index factor required to convert to January 20X0 values.

3.   In the third column, calculate the monthly sales in January 20X0 terms (to the nearest £1,000).

FOULKS LYNCH
PUBLICATIONS

TASK 4

MANUFACTURERS AND PRODUCERS ASSOCIATION
17 Pharaoh Street, Gadtown GW3 1QR

Dear Member

Please supply the following information for your most recent accounting period.

The information should be prepared in accordance with the notes below.

Name of company   _____

Membership number   _____

Financial year end   _____

1   Turnover for the year   _____

    Percentage change on previous year (+/-)   _____

2   Production costs as percentage of sales   _____

3   Administration costs as percentage of sales   _____

4   Distribution costs as percentage of sales   _____

5   Gross profit percentage   _____

6   Net profit percentage   _____

7   Return on capital employed   _____

Notes

1.   Turnover should be stated net of VAT.

2.   Return on capital employed should be calculated as the proportion of net profit to total capital employed, expressed as a percentage.

3.   Percentages and ratios should be stated to two decimal places.

Please return the completed form to Leah Laban at the above address by 31 January 20X5.

Thank you for your assistance.

TASK 6

HM Customs and Excise

Value Added Tax Return
For the period
01-10-X4 **to** 31-12-X4

For Official Use

Registration number	Period
570 4060 19	12 X4

You could be liable to a financial penalty if your completed return and all the VAT payable are not received by the due date.

Due date: 31.01.X5

⌐　　　　　　　　　　　¬

JACOB LIMITED
UNIT 7
THAMESVIEW BUSINESS PARK
CULTHAM
CM5 8RW

L　　　　　　　　　　　⌐

For official use D O R only	

Fold Here

Before you fill in this form please read the notes on the back and the VAT leaflet *"Filling in your VAT return"*. Fill all boxes clearly in ink, and write 'none' where necessary. Don't put a dash or leave any box blank. If there are no pence write "00" in the pence column. Do **not** enter more than one amount in any box.

			£	p
For official use	VAT due in this period on **sales** and other outputs	**1**		
	VAT due in this period on **acquisitions** from other **EC Member States**	**2**		
	Total VAT due (**the sum of boxes 1 and 2**)	**3**		
	VAT reclaimed in this period on **purchases** and other inputs (including acquisitions from the EC)	**4**		
	Net VAT to be paid to Customs or reclaimed by you (**Difference between boxes 3 and 4**)	**5**		
	Total value of **sales** and all other outputs excluding any VAT. **Include your box 8 figure**	**6**		00
	Total value of **purchases** and all other inputs excluding any VAT. **Include your box 9 figure**	**7**		00
	Total value of **all supplies** of goods and related services, excluding any VAT, to other **EC Member States**	**8**		00
	Total value of all **acquisitions** of goods and related services, excluding any VAT, from other **EC Member States**	**9**		00

If you are enclosing a payment please tick this box	DECLARATION: You, or someone on your behalf, must sign below.
	I, ... declare that the
	(Full name of signatory in BLOCK LETTERS)
	information given above is true and complete.
☐	Signature .... Date ....
	A false declaration can result in prosecution

PRACTICE SIMULATION 6

COVERAGE OF PERFORMANCE CRITERIA

The following performance criteria are covered in this simulation, in the tasks noted

Element	PC Coverage	Task(s)
7.1	**Prepare and present periodic performance reports**	
A	Consolidate information derived from different units of the organisation into the appropriate form.	1
B	Reconcile information derived from different information systems within the organisation.	1, 6
C	Compare results over time using an appropriate method that allows for changing price levels.	3
D	Account for transactions between separate units of the organisation in accordance with the organisation's procedures.	1
E	Calculate ratios and performance indicators in accordance with the organisation's procedures.	5
F	Prepare reports in the appropriate form and present them to management within the required timescales.	2, 5
7.2	**Prepare reports and returns for outside agencies**	
A	Identify, collate and present relevant information in accordance with the	4
B	Conventions and definitions used by outside agencies. Ensure calculations of ratios and performance indicators are accurate.	4
C	Obtain authorisation for the despatch of completed reports and returns from the appropriate person.	5
D	Presented reports and returns in accordance with outside agencies' requirements and deadlines.	4
7.3	**Prepare VAT returns**	
A	Complete and submit VAT returns correctly, using data from the appropriate recording systems, within the statutory time limits.	6
B	Correctly identify and calculate relevant inputs and outputs.	6
C	Ensure submissions are made in accordance with current legislation.	6, 8
D	Ensure guidance is sought from the VAT office when required, in a professional manner.	7

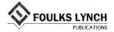

THE SITUATION

You are a qualified accounting technician working as an accounts clerk for Albion Manufacturing Limited. You report to the company's accountant, Amanda Buckley.

The business and structure of Albion Manufacturing Limited

The business of Albion Manufacturing Limited is the manufacture and sale of electronic sound mixers to the audio and recording industry. The business is structured in three divisions:

- The manufacturing division buys in electronic components and other materials and uses them to manufacture printed circuit boards (PSBs).

- The assembly division receives PCBs from the manufacturing division and buys in other materials from external suppliers. The division then assembles these components to form finished goods.

- The sales and administration division receives finished mixers from the assembly division and sells them to customers. This division is also responsible for all of the administration and establishment functions within the company.

The business of the company is conducted from a single site in the town of Throstles, comprising a factory complex (housing the manufacturing and assembly divisions) and a combined office and warehouse block (housing the sales and administration division, as well as a finished goods storage area). You may assume throughout the simulation that work in progress stocks are negligible. Finished goods stocks are transferred from Assembly to Sales and Administration with delay.

Accounts and reports

Direct costs of manufacture and assembly are attributed to the manufacturing and assembly divisions respectively. These divisions also bear the factory overhead costs, allocated between the divisions in a predetermined ratio.

Administration and establishment costs, including the salaries of administration and selling staff, are attributed to the sales and administration division.

All transfers between divisions are accounted for at cost (in other words, there is no inter-divisional profit).

At the end of the accounting year (31 December) the summary cost statements for the manufacturing and assembly divisions, and the summary cost and revenue statements for the sales and administration division, are consolidated in a standard form to produce a global statement of costs and revenue.

Cost Statement: Manufacturing Division
Year Ended 31 December 20X3

Raw materials	£
Opening stock	24,217
Purchases	175,632
	199,849
Closing, stock	30,071
Total usage	169,778
Factory labour	124,561
Factory overheads	88,903
Transfer cost to assembly division	383,242

Cost Statement: Assembly Division
Year Ended 31 December 20X3

Raw materials	£
Opening stock	19,764
Purchases	96,452
	383,242
Closing stock	499,458
	27,614
Total usage	471,844
Factory labour	117,410
Factory overheads	126,732
Transfer cost to sales and administration division*	715,986

*Representing the cost of 52 completed mixers transferred.

Cost and Revenue Statement: Sales and Administration Division

Year Ended 31 December 20X3

Sales	£	£
Cost of finished goods sold		1,452,317
Opening stock	52,081	
Transfer price from assembly division	715,986	
	768,067	
Closing stock	39,612	
	728,455	
Sales and administration salaries	207,514	
Other admin and establishment costs	247,091	
Total costs		1,183,060
Net profit before taxation		269,257

Consolidated Statement Of Cost and Revenues for the

Year Ended 31 December 20X2

Sales	£	£
Cost of sales		1,304,723
Materials	248,501	
Factory labour	239,550	
Factory overhead	213,452	
Movement in stock of finished goods	(13,761)	
		687,742
Gross profit		616,981
Sales and administration salaries		199,502
Other admin and establishment costs		228,787
Net profit before tax		188,692

FOULKS LYNCH
PUBLICATIONS

MEMORANDUM

To: Accounts Clerk

From: Amanda Buckley

Date: 17 January 20X4

Subject: Results for 20X3

I have a paper to prepare for the Board meeting on 25 January concerning the financial results for 20X3.

The Board will be looking at the figures for 20X3 in comparison with the adjusted figures for 2001 which I know you have been working on. What I would like from you is:

- Firstly, a note of any significant improvements or deteriorations in revenue or costs. Don't bother about items where the change has been trivial, but where there has been a marked variation between the 20X3 figure and the adjusted figure for 20X2 please mention it so that I can start looking for explanations

- Secondly, some kind of diagrammatic breakdown of how our total sales revenue is absorbed. I don't want my Board paper to look too dull, so perhaps you could come up with a bar chart showing the percentages of revenue represented by factory costs, sales, administration and establishment costs, and profit. If you could do that for both the 20X3 results and the adjusted 20X2 results it would be very helpful.

Could I ask for all of this by close of business on Friday 19 January please?

Thanks

Amanda

THE TASKS TO BE COMPLETED

TASK 1   Above you will find accounting statements for the year ended 31 December 20X3, namely, cost statements for the manufacturing and assembly divisions of Albion Manufacturing Limited, cost and revenue statement for the sales and administration division.

Calculate the total production cost per unit of finished goods transferred from assembly to sales and administration during the year ended 31 December 20X3 and the ratio of total factory overheads to total factory salaries for the year.

TASK 2   Prepare a consolidated statement of costs and revenues for the company as a whole for the year ended 31 December 20X3.

TASK 3   The management of Albion have made the following estimates relating to the effect of price inflation on the accounting figures for the year ended 31 December 20X3.

- Materials costs have been on average 4% more expensive than in 20X2.

- Factory labour and overhead costs have been on average 3% more expensive.

- Sales, administration and establishment costs have been on average 4% more expensive

- Albion's own sales prices have risen by 5% on average.

You are required, on the basis of these estimates, to re-state in 20X3 terms the consolidated figures of costs and revenues for the year ended 31 December 20X2. Then calculate the percentage increase or decrease achieved in sales, cost of sales and net profit in 20X3 compared with the adjusted figures for 20X2.

TASK 4   Prepare a reply (in the form of a memo) to Amanda Buckley's memo reproduced above

TASK 5

Below is an extract from a standard form, issued by a grant authority responsible for processing Albion's grant applications. Insert the accounting figures ratios and statistics required by the authority. Your answer should be based on consolidated figure (not divisional figures) and should include only actual (not price adjusted) amounts.

Financial Information in Support of Application

(extracts)

Name of company ....

Year ended...

Data ....

	Current year £	% of sales	Previous year £	% of sales
Sales				
Gross profit				
Net profit before taxation				
Total labour and salary costs (A)				
Production costs not included in (A)				
Other costs				

TASK 6

Write a memo to Amanda Buckley asking for authorisation to send the form you completed in Task 6 to John Kay, who is responsible for submitting the application for a grant.

FOULKS LYNCH
PUBLICATIONS

ANSWERS TO PRACTICE ACTIVITIES

BASIC MATHEMATICAL TECHNIQUES

ACTIVITY 1

Price	Quantity	Price × Quantity
10	50	500
12	100	1,200
14	40	560
16	20	320
	210	2,580

Weighted average of prices $= \dfrac{2,580}{210}$ (£)

$= £12.29$

ACTIVITY 2

	Product A Budget £	Product A Actual £	% Change	Product B Budget £	Product B Actual £	% Change
Sales	98,000	103,000	+ 5.1	14,000	20,000	+42.9
Material costs	(34,000)	(39,000)	+14 7	(4,600)	(7,200)	+56.5
Labour costs	(24,200)	(23,600)	− 2.5	(2,650)	(2,650)	0
Overheads	(24,200)	(20,000)	−17.4	(2,650)	(3,400)	+28.3
Contribution	15,600	20,400	+30.8	4,100	6,750	+64.6

TABULATION OF DATA

ACTIVITY 3

Alpha Products plc
Changes in labour force 20X7 to 20X8

	Department A			Department B			Total		
	20X7	20X8	Change %	20X7	20X8	Change %	20X7	20X8	Change %
Wage bill (£'000)	218	224	+2.8	295	313	+6.1	513	537	+4.7
Number employed	30	25	−16.7	42	43	+2.4	72	68	−5.6

ACTIVITY 4

Waterson plc – Profit for the period 20X8 to 20X9						
	Property division			Manufacturing division		
	20X8	20X9	Increase %	20X8	20X9	Increase %
Pre-tax profits (£'000)	12,141	15,426	27	8,343	9,271	11
Earnings per share (pence)	24.10	29.62	23	14.91	15.75	6
Dividend per share (pence)	11.52	13.50	17	8.86	9.63	9
Percentage total group profits	59	62		41	38	

Tutorial note:

The table shows that the property division performed better than the manufacturing division in every respect.

The increase in earnings and dividends per share for the manufacturing division are probably not much above the general rate of inflation and therefore achieved practically no growth in real terms. The proportion of total contribution to profits by the property division is greater than that of the manufacturing division and is increasing.

ACTIVITY 5

Highest value is 199 cm, lowest value is 167 cm; therefore, range of values = 32 cm.

Taking class intervals as 165 cm and less than 170 cm, 170 cm and less than 175 cm, etc. the distribution becomes:

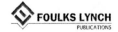

Class interval		Frequency
Height (cms)	Tally	Number of students
165 and less than 170	IIII	5
170 and less than 175	III1	4
175 and less than 180	IIII III	8
180 and less than 185	IIII IIII IIII-1	16
185 and less than 190	IIII I	6
190 and less than 195	IIII I1	7
195 and less than 200	III1	4
Total		50

Note: Take each item in the original table of raw data in the order in which it appears and place a tally mark in the appropriate class. That is, take 174 and put a tally mark against 170 and less than 175 cms. Then take 196 and put a tally mark against 195 and less than 200 cms. Do not go through the raw data picking out all the items in the first class, then go through it all again picking out all the items in the second class, etc. as this is much more time consuming and is more prone to mistakes.

ACTIVITY 6

The smallest value in the distribution is 105, the largest value in the distribution is 142. The range to be spanned is 142 – 105, i.e. 37. The following grouping is a suggestion. The classes should be of equal width.

Group	Tally	Frequency
105 but less than 110	II	2
110 but less than 115	IIII	5
115 but less than 120	IIII	4
120 but less than 125	IIII III	8
125 but less than 130	IIII IIII	10
130 but less than 135	IIII	5
135 but less than 140	IIII	4
140 but less than 145	II	2
Total		40

ACTIVITY 7

UK Merchant Fleet 20X3 to 20X5

Type of vessel	Number of vessels				Gross tonnage ('000)			
			Change				Change	
	20X3	20X5	Actual	%	20X3	20X5	Actual	%
Passenger	86	85	−1	−1.2	573	626	+53	+9.2
Tanker	329	257	−72	−21.9	10,030	6,812	−3,218	−32.1
Cargo liner	134	97	−37	−27.6	1,194	876	−318	−26.6
Container	64	55	−9	−14.1	1,613	1,559	−54	−3.3
Tramp	190	167	−23	−12.1	406	352	−54	−13.3
Bulk carrier	128	80	−48	−37.5	4,709	3,109	−1,600	−34.0
Total	931	741	−190	−20.4	18,525	13,334	−5,191	−28.0

Note: All data is for the month of April in each year.

Tutorial note: Percentages are not additive. Thus the total percentage in column 5 cannot be obtained by adding the percentages above it. It must be calculated from the actual change (−190) expressed as a percentage of the first total (931).

DIAGRAMMATIC PRESENTATION

ACTIVITY 8

Pie charts

Workings

Angles required to represent the given data for the two years are as follows:

	20X6	Degrees	20X7	Degrees
United Kingdom	1,760	209	1,800	171
EC countries (other than UK)	576	68	612	58
Other European countries	214	25	374	35
North and South America	306	36	354	34
CIS	54	7	72	7
Other overseas countries	127	15	584	55
	3,037	360	3,796	360

Analysis of sales by market in 20X6

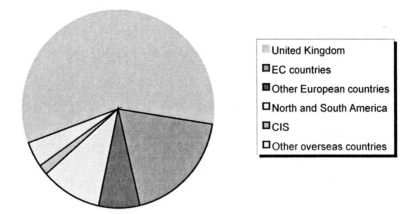

Analysis of sales by markets in 20X7

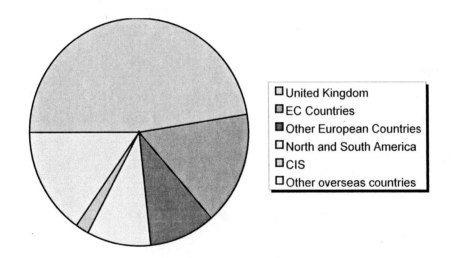

ACTIVITY 9

Component bar charts

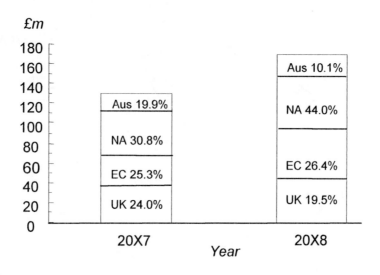

Annual sales 20X7 to 20X8

Tutorial notes

(1)   Once the chart has been completed the left-hand scale can be erased.

(2)   If there is no room to write the details in each section, use shading and a key.

ACTIVITY 10

Multiple bar chart

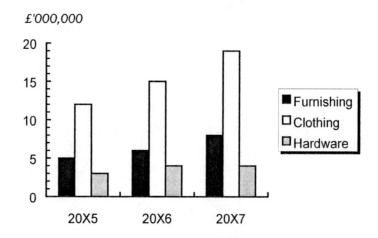

Departmental sales 20X5 to 20X7

ACTIVITY 11

(a) Before drawing any diagram it is necessary to calculate the actual sales by product groups, as only the percentage sales are given in the question.

For 20X5   £m

Product A   24% of 6.3 = $\dfrac{24}{100} \times 6.3 =$ 1.51

Product B   12% of 6.3 = $\dfrac{12}{100} \times 6.3 =$ 0.76

Product C   16% of 6.3 = $\dfrac{16}{100} \times 6.3 =$ 1.01

Others   48% of 6.3 = $\dfrac{48}{100} \times 6.3 =$ 3.02

                                                                        ____

Total   6.30
                                                                        ____

Similar calculations are necessary for the years 20X4 to 20X1 inclusive.

Showing this in a tabular form gives:

Sales in £ million

Product	20X5	20X4	20X3	20X2	20X1
A	1.51	1.43	1.16	0.94	0.58
B	0.76	0.65	0.64	0.42	0.47
C	1.01	1.37	1.33	1.22	1.17
Others	3.02	3.05	2.67	2.12	1.68
Total	6.30	6.50	5.80	4.70	3.90

This information can now be displayed in a bar chart.

Sales by product groups, 20X1 to 20X5

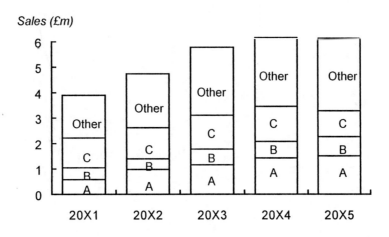

(b)   In order to analyse the total sales for each of the two years 20X4 and 20X5, it is necessary to consider the relative proportions of cost, taxation and profit.

Years

	20X4			*20X5*		
Direct materials	$\frac{3.2}{6.5} \times 100 =$	49.2%		$\frac{3.1}{6.3} \times 100 =$	49.2%	
Direct wages	$\frac{1.2}{6.5} \times 100 =$	18.5%		$\frac{1.4}{6.3} \times 100 =$	22.2%	
Production overhead	$\frac{1.0}{6.5} \times 100 =$	15.4%		$\frac{1.0}{6.3} \times 100 =$	15.9%	
Other overhead	$\frac{0.4}{6.5} \times 100 =$	6.2%		$\frac{0.4}{6.3} \times 100 =$	6.3%	
Taxation	$\frac{0.3}{6.5} \times 100 =$	4.6%		$\frac{0.3}{6.3} \times 100 =$	4.8%	
Profit	$\frac{0.4}{6.5} \times 100 =$	6.2%		$\frac{0.1}{6.3} \times 100 =$	1.6%	
Totals		100.1%			100.0%	

(due to rounding)

This information can now be best expressed in two pie charts.

In order to calculate the angles of the sectors, remember 100% is represented by 360° therefore, every 1% is represented by 3.6°.

Analysis of costs, taxation and profit 20X4

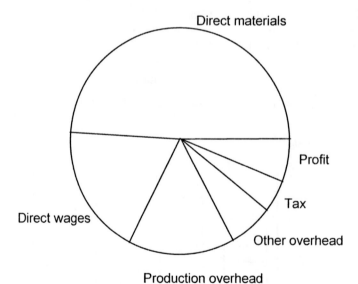

FOULKS LYNCH
PUBLICATIONS

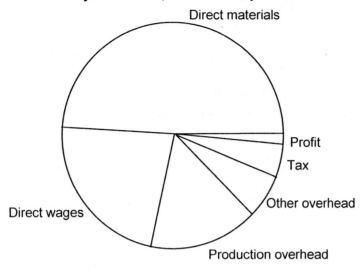

Analysis of costs, taxation and profit 20X5

To emphasise direct wages, this sector could be 'exploded', i.e. shown as if partially separated from the rest of the pie, or shaded more heavily than the other sectors

Comments

The most noticeable differences between the two years are:

(i) *Direct wages* – these have risen from 18.5% of sales in 20X4 to 22.2% of sales in 20X5. An increase of 3.7%.

(ii) *Profit* – this has fallen from 6.2% of sales in 20X4 to 1.6% of sales in 20X5. A decrease of 4.6%.

All other percentages compare very favourably – 0.5% being the largest difference apart from those noted above.

The increase in direct wages, etc. in 20X5 has resulted in a fall in profits. (This is true in absolute and relative terms.)

GRAPHICAL PRESENTATION

ACTIVITY 12

Month	20X7/20X8	20X8/20X9	Cumulative total 20X8/20X9	Moving annual total 20X8/20X9
June	600	700	700	7,800
July	500	600	1,300	7,900
August	600	600	1,900	7,900
September	600	700	2,600	8,000
October	700	900	3,500	8,200
November	800	1,000	4,500	8,400
December	900	1,000	5,500	8,500
January	600	700	6,200	8,600
February	400	500	6,700	8,700
March	600	700	7,400	8,800
April	600	700	8,100	8,900
May	800	900	9,000	9,000

Tutorial note: The moving annual total is the total for 12 months up to and including the current month, hence:

Moving annual total for June 20X9 = Total from July 20X8 to June 20X9 inclusive

Moving annual total for July 20X9 = Moving annual total for previous month − 500 + 600, etc.

Note that the final moving annual total value must equal the final cumulative total value.

Z chart of sales, AT Photographic Company June 20X8 to May 20X9

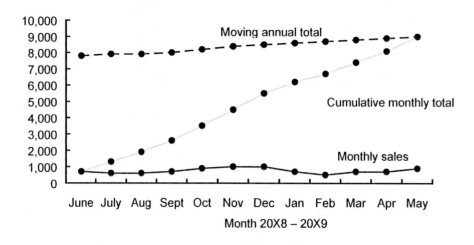

ACTIVITY 13

Arrange in numerical order:

501, 502, 503, 504, 504, 504, 505, 505, 506, 506, 507, 508

(a) (i) The median weight is $\dfrac{504+505}{2}$ = 504.5 kg.

(ii) The modal weight is 504 kg (it occurs three times).

(iii) To make calculating the arithmetic mean easier subtract 500.

Mean = 500 + $\dfrac{1+2+3+4+4+4+5+5+6+6+7+8}{12}$

= 500 + $\dfrac{55}{12}$

= 504.58 kg

FOULKS LYNCH
PUBLICATIONS

ACTIVITY 14

(a) & (b)   **Scattergraph of advertising expenditure and newspaper circulation**

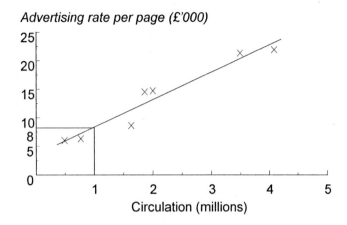

(c)   Using the graph above, the approximate advertising rate per page for an expected circulation of 1 million would be £8,000.

ACTIVITY 15

(a)   ***Tutorial note:*** The range of values is from 1.7 to 9.0. A convenient number of groups will therefore be 10, from 0–1, 1–2, etc. but choose the intervals so that there is no ambiguity about boundary values. As the data is continuous, there must be no gaps between the group boundaries.

Grouped frequency table

Time (minutes)	Tally	Frequency
0 and less than 1		0
1 and less than 2	I	1
2 and less than 3	II	2
3 and less than 4	III	3
4 and less than 5	IIII	5
5 and less than 6	IIII IIII	10
6 and less than 7	IIII I	6
7 and less than 8	IIII	4
8 and less than 9	III	3
9 and less than 10	I	1
Total		35

(b) **Histogram of times to complete operation**

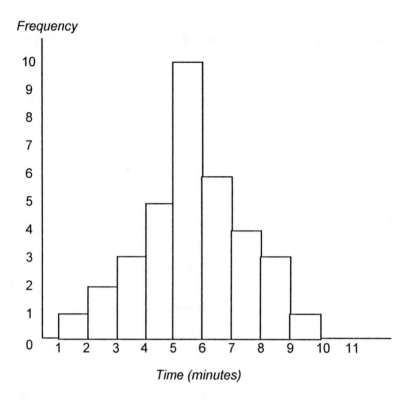

ACTIVITY 16

(a) & (b) **Histogram and frequency polygon**

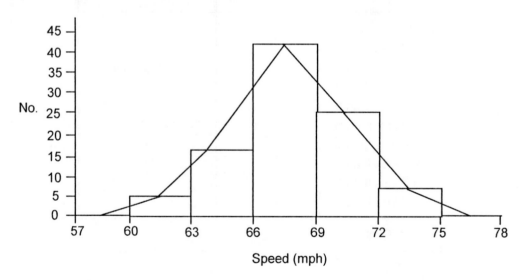

Note: the frequency polygon is achieved by joining up the mid-points of the histogram. Note the correct treatment of the two ends of the polygon.

ACTIVITY 17

Find the mid point of each class interval, x, and produce a table showing x, f and f multiplied by x (fx).

Multiply (x) by (f) and calculate the sum of fx.

Mid-value	Frequency	
x	f	fx
155	1	155
165	9	1,485
175	12	2,100
185	16	2,960
195	26	5,070
205	19	3,895
215	8	1,720
225	6	1,350
235	2	470
245	1	245
Totals	(Sum of)Σf = 100	(Sum of)Σfx = 19,450

Calculate the arithmetic mean.

The arithmetic mean $= \dfrac{\Sigma fx}{\Sigma f} = \dfrac{19,450}{100} = 194.5$ cms

Notice that, if the original data had units so the mean should have units.

It might be worth practising calculating means on your scientific calculator.

ACTIVITY 18

(a) A frequency distribution of photocopying times with six classes:

Class	Tally	Frequency (No. of uses)
0.0 to under 2.0	⪡ ‖	7
2.0 to under 4.0	⪡ ‖‖	9
4.0 to under 6.0	⪡ ⪡ ⪡ ‖	16
6.0 to under 8.0	⪡ ⪡ ⪡	15
8.0 to under 10.0	⪡ ‖‖	8
10.0 to under 12.0	⪡	5
Total		60

The frequency distribution is almost bell-shaped, symmetrical, having a slight positive skewness.

(b)   **Histogram: To show photocopier use**

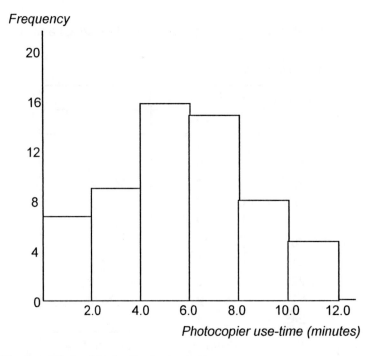

(c)   The modal class is 4 - 6 minutes.

It tells us that the most frequent time span spent by a user at the photocopier is 4 to 6 minutes.

(d)

Class	Class midpoint x	Frequency f	fx
0 – < 2	1.0	7	7
2 – < 4	3.0	9	27
4 – < 6	5.0	16	80
6 – < 8	7.0	15	105
8 – < 10	9.0	8	72
10 – < 12	11.0	5	55
		60	346

Mean use-time = $\dfrac{346}{60}$ = 5.77 minutes

TIME SERIES ANALYSIS

ACTIVITY 19

(a) & (b)   **Appliance sales 20X1 to 20X9**

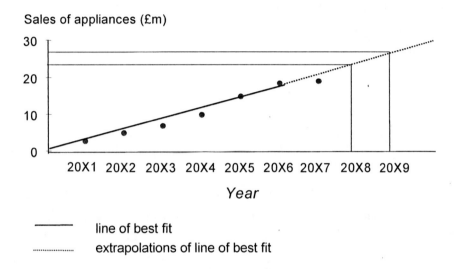

Sales of appliances (£m)

——— line of best fit

.... extrapolations of line of best fit

Forecast appliance sales for 20X8 are £23 million and for 20X9 are £26 million

(c)   **Policy sales and appliance sales**

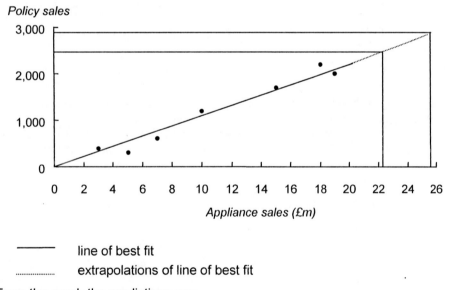

——— line of best fit

.... extrapolations of line of best fit

(d)   From the graph the predictions are:

20X8 Sales £23m   Policies 2,500

20X9 Sales £26m   Policies 2,800

Both graphs are subject to error due to the scatter in the points, but the scatter is
sufficiently contained to suggest that a linear relationship is justified in both cases.
However, both predictions are based on extrapolations which assume the linear
relationship is going to continue in the future. There is no guarantee that this will be

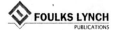

the case. Bearing this in mind, the forecasts would be sufficiently accurate to be useful for planning purposes, but the forecasts for 20X9 will be less reliable than those for 20X8, as the extrapolation was made over a longer time period.

ACTIVITY 20

(a)   Seasonal variation – high in summer, low in winter

(b)   Rising trend

(c)   Seasonal variation – high in autumn/winter, low in summer

(d)   Cyclical variation (affected by booms and depressions)

(e)   Decreasing trend

(f)   Residual (random) variation

ACTIVITY 21

(a)

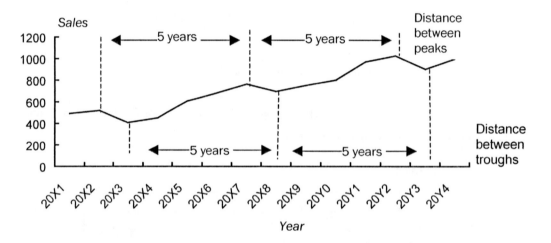

(b)   In order to calculate the trend figures it is necessary to establish the span of the cycle. From the graph it can easily be seen that the distance in time between successive peaks (and successive troughs) is five years; therefore a five-point moving average must be calculated. No other type of average will smooth out the five yearly cycle of fluctuations.

A table of the following form is now drawn up:

Year	Sales £'000	Five yearly moving total	Five yearly moving average
20X1	491	–	–
20X2	519	–	–
20X3	407	2,476	495
20X4	452	2,666	533
20X5	607	2,911	582
20X6	681	3,200	640
20X7	764	3,499	700
20X8	696	3,694	739
20X9	751	3,983	797
20Y0	802	4,245	849
20Y1	970	4,452	890
20Y2	1,026	4,699	940
20Y3	903	–	–
20Y4	998	–	–

Tutorial notes on the calculation

(i)   As the name implies, the five yearly moving total is the sum of successive groups of five years' sales, i.e.:

491 + 519 + 407 + 452 + 607   = 2,476

Then advancing by one year:

519 + 407 + 452 + 607 + 681   = 2,666, etc. until, for the last five years

802 + 970 + 1,026 + 903 + 998   = 4,699

It is not necessary to add five values each time. For the second total, 491 is omitted and 681 included instead, hence the total will increase by 190. Similarly, for the third total omit 519 and include 764, an increase of 245 and so on.

(ii)   These moving totals are simply divided by five to give the moving averages, i.e.:

2,476 ÷ 5 = 495

2,666 ÷ 5 = 533

|
|
|

4,699 ÷ 5 = 940

(iii)   Averages are always plotted in the middle of the time period, i.e. 495 is the average of the figures for 20X1, 20X2, 20X3, 20X4 and 20X5 and so it is plotted at the end of 20X3, this being the mid-point of the time interval from the end of 20X1 to the end of 20X5. Similarly, 533 is plotted at the end of 19X4 and 940 is plotted at the end of 20Y2.

A second graph is now drawn showing the original figures again and the trend figures, i.e. the five yearly moving averages.

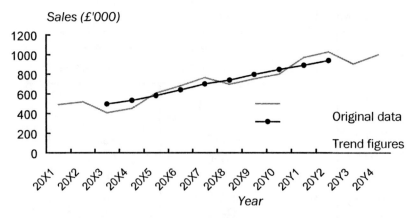

Note how the fluctuations have been smoothed out. This is only achieved if each average is calculated over a complete cycle, in this example a five yearly one.

ACTIVITY 22

Malcan plc

(a)

Day	Output A	Five day total (centred on the middle day)	Trend T
Monday	187		
Tuesday	203		
Wednesday	208	1,022	204
Thursday	207	1,042	208
Friday	217	1,047	209
Monday	207	1,049	210
Tuesday	208	1,048	210
Wednesday	210	1,043	209
Thursday	206	1,038	208
Friday	212	1,040	208
Monday	202	1,042	208
Tuesday	210	1,041	208
Wednesday	212	1,043	209
Thursday	205	1,049	210
Friday	214	1,054	211
Monday	208	1,059	212
Tuesday	215	1,071	214
Wednesday	217	1,070	214
Thursday	217		
Friday	213		

Note that in calculating the trend, which is the average of the five day total, it is centred on the third day in every group of five because the cycle consists of an odd number of periods.

(b)   **Malcan plc: Production Output**

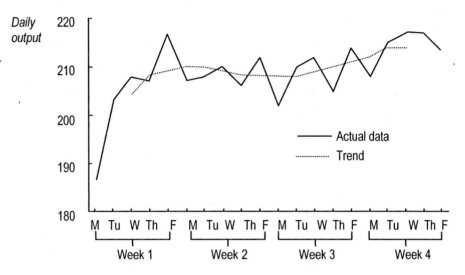

INDEX NUMBERS

ACTIVITY 23

Year	Price index	Quantity index
20X1	100	100
20X2	$\dfrac{125}{120} \times 100 = 104.2$	$\dfrac{5.2}{5.3} \times 100 = 98.1$
20X3	$\dfrac{131}{120} \times 100 = 109.2$	$\dfrac{5.0}{5.3} \times 100 = 94.3$

Tutorial Comments

The price increased by 4.2% from 20X1 to 20X2 and by 9.2% in the two year period from 20X1 to 20X3. Sales quantities decreased by 1.9% from 20X1 to 20X2 and by 5.7% in the two year period from 20X1 to 20X3. Thus as price increased, quantity sold decreased. This does not necessarily mean that increase in price was the direct cause of the decrease in sales. Other factors such as inflation or economic depression could cause sales to fall although generally there is an inverse relationship between sales and price.

ACTIVITY 24

Indexed sales to external customers

Manufacturing and Distribution divisions combined

	Unadjusted totals £'000	Index factor	Indexed totals £'000
20X3			
January	366	0.905	331
February	228	0.911	208
March	229	0.903	207
April	316	0.899	284
May	308	0.898	276
June	284	0.895	254
July	222	0.897	199
August	342	0.896	306
September	330	0.894	295
October	292	0.893	261
November	266	0.890	237
December	358	0.887	318

ACTIVITY 25

Year	Sales	Fixed base index (20X1 = 100)	Chain base index	
20X1	£1,000	100		100
20X2	£1,100	110.0	$\frac{110}{100} \times 100$	110
20X3	£1,210	121.0	$\frac{121}{110} \times 100$	110
20X4	£1,331	133.1	$\frac{133.1}{121} \times 100$	110
20X5	£1,464	146.4	$\frac{146.4}{133.1} \times 100$	110

Note: Chain base index for year n = $\dfrac{\text{Fixed base index for year n}}{\text{Fixed base index for previous year}} \times 100$

Although the sales of radios have increased each year, the chain base index numbers have remained static at 110. Therefore, the annual rate of increase of sales of radios is remaining constant rather than increasing.

Tutorial note: Do not confuse *rate* of increase with *actual* increase. Actual sales are increasing each year but the rate of increase is constant at 10% per year.

PERFORMANCE INDICATORS

ACTIVITY 26

			20X3	20X2

(a)

(i) Net profit on sales

$$\frac{35,000}{200,000} \times 100 \qquad \frac{30,000}{120,000} \times 100$$

$$= 17.5\% \qquad\qquad = 25\%$$

(ii) Gross profit on sales

$$\frac{50,000}{200,000} \times 100 \qquad \frac{40,000}{120,000} \times 100$$

$$= 25\% \qquad\qquad = 33.3\%$$

(iii) Return on capital employed

$$\frac{35,000}{41,000} \times 100 \qquad \frac{30,000}{29,000} \times 100$$

$$= 85.4\% \qquad\qquad = 103.4\%$$

(iv) Debtor collection period

$$\frac{36,000}{200,000} \times 365 \qquad \frac{12,000}{120,000} \times 365$$

$$= 66 \text{ days} \qquad\qquad = 37 \text{ days}$$

(v) Current ratio

$$\frac{54,000}{25,000} \qquad\qquad \frac{20,000}{6,000}$$

$$= 2.2 \qquad\qquad = 3.3$$

(vi) Acid test (or quick) ratio

$$\frac{54,000 - 18,000}{25,000} \qquad \frac{20,000 - 7,000}{6,000}$$

$$= 1.4 \qquad\qquad = 2.2$$

(b) It is suggested that as an apparent result of a reduction in Free's selling prices during 20X2/X3, the following points could be made:

(i) Free's sales have increased by £80,000 (66.7%).

(ii) The gross profit has increased by £10,000 (25%) and the net profit by £5,000 (16.7%). The net profit has probably been affected by an increase in fixed costs (up from £10,000 in 20X2 to £15,000 in 20X3) as a result of the increase in sales.

(iii) As a result of the reduction in selling prices the gross profit margin has also fallen sharply – from 33.3% in 20X2 to 25% in 20X3. This is, of course, to be expected.

(iv) Free's return on capital employed still remains remarkably high, falling from 103.4% in 20X2 to 85.4% in 20X3 but note that these returns have been calculated on year end balances. Since Free has also drawn substantially from the business (£13,000 in 20X2 but rising to £23,000 in 20X3), the capital employed at the end of the year appears correspondingly smaller.

(v) A much longer period of credit has been granted – up from an average of 37 days in 20X2 to an average of 66 days in 20X3. Alternatively, it may be that Free has not been able to cope with the increase in sales and the debtor control system has broken down. Whatever the reason, it has converted a favourable bank balance of £1,000 at the end of 20X2 to an overdrawn one of £10,000 at the end of 20X3.

(vi) It would appear that Free's liquidity position in 20X3 as measured by both the current ratio (2.2) and the acid test (or quick) ratio (1.4) is satisfactory, although the situation has deteriorated since 20X2 when the ratios were 3.3 and 2.2 respectively. In fact, although Free is trading successfully and the profit margins are high, the cash flow is at a critical level. This is sometimes known as *over-trading*.

Free ought to insist that the trade debtors settle their debts more quickly than they appear to have been doing in 20X3. Otherwise it may be necessary to reduce cash drawings since these have helped to exacerbate the cash position during the current year.

ACTIVITY 27

(a) **Gross profit percentage**

$$\frac{\text{Gross profit}}{\text{Sales}} \times 100 \quad = \quad \frac{50,000}{100,000} \times 100 \quad = \quad 50\%$$

(b) **Net profit percentage**

$$\frac{\text{Net profit}}{\text{Sales}} \times 100 \quad = \quad \frac{25,000}{100,000} \times 100 \quad = \quad 25\%$$

(c) **Return on capital employed**

$$\frac{\text{Net profit}}{\text{Capital}} \times 100 \quad = \quad \frac{25,000}{33,000} \times 100 \quad = \quad 75.8\%$$

(d) **Stock turnover**

$$\frac{\text{Cost of goods sold}}{\text{Closing stock}} \quad = \quad \frac{50,000}{12,000} \quad = \quad 4.2 \text{ times pa}$$

or

$$\frac{\text{Cost of goods sold}}{\text{Average stock}} \quad = \quad \frac{50,000}{(10,000+12,000) \div 2} \quad = \quad 4.5 \text{ times pa}$$

(e) **Debtor collection period**

$$\frac{\text{Trade debtors}}{\text{Credit sales}} \times 365 \quad = \quad \frac{7,000}{100,000} \times 365 \quad = \quad 26 \text{ days}$$

(f) **Current ratio**

$$\frac{\text{Current assets}}{\text{Current liabilities}} \quad = \quad \frac{20,000}{5,000} \quad = \quad 4$$

(g) **Quick (or acid test) ratio**

$$\frac{\text{Current assets} - \text{Stocks}}{\text{Current liabilities}} \quad = \quad \frac{20,000 - 12,000}{5,000} \quad = \quad 1.6$$

ACTIVITY 28

A to B Railway Company Ltd has been successful in increasing in real terms its receipts in relation to the distances covered. This does not mean that its total receipts have increased. The business may well have cut back on railway lines that were not economically viable.

It has not been successful in controlling its costs measured on the same basis as receipts and therefore the net effect of 41 and 42 is broadly neutral.

Productivity of staff has increased significantly. Items 43 and 45 both indicate this.

Wage costs are presumably a significant element of total costs. The relationship of sales revenue to wages costs has improved slightly.

Item 46 indicates that A to B Railway Company Ltd is using its track more efficiently or that it has removed lines which were uneconomic to run (i.e. few trips were made on them). This is supporting evidence of the comments made on item 41.

ACTIVITY 29

(a) **Room occupancy**

$$\frac{\text{Total number of rooms occupied}}{\text{Rooms available to be let}} = \frac{200+30}{240+40} = 82.1\%$$

(b) **Bed occupancy**

$$\frac{\text{Total number of beds occupied}}{\text{Total number of beds available}} = \frac{6{,}450 \text{ guests} \times 2 \text{ days per guest}}{[(240\times2)+(40\times1)]\times30 \text{ days}}$$

$$= \frac{12{,}900}{15{,}600} = 82.7\%$$

(c) **Average guest rate**

$$\frac{\text{Total revenue}}{\text{Number of guests}} = \frac{£774{,}000}{6{,}450} = £120$$

(d) **Revenue utilisation**

$$\frac{\text{Actual revenue}}{\text{Maximum revenue from available rooms}} = \frac{£774{,}000}{[(240\times£110)+(40\times£70)]\times30 \text{ days}}$$

$$= \frac{£774{,}000}{£876{,}000} = 88.4\%$$

(e) **Cost of cleaning supplies per occupied room per day**

$$\frac{£5{,}000}{(200+30)\times30 \text{ days}} = £0.7$$

(f) **Average cost per occupied bed**

$$\frac{\text{Total cost}}{\text{Number of beds occupied}} = \frac{£100{,}000+£5{,}000+£22{,}500}{6{,}450\times2}$$

$$= £9.9$$

WRITING REPORTS

ACTIVITY 30

MEMORANDUM

To: Roger Byrne

Form: Accounting Technician

Subject: Rations and performance indicators for 20X4

Date: 13 January 20X5

Here are the required ratios and performance indicators for the year 31 December 20X4:

Gross profit percentage:

$$(£3,541,000 – £2,070,000)/ £3,541,000 = 41.54\%$$

Net profit percentage:

$$£1,471,000 – £523,000 – £401,000 – £151,000)/$$
$$£3,541,000 = 11.18\%$$

Production cost per unit produced
and sold in the year:

$$£2,070,000/ 181,000 = £11.44$$

The value of sales earned per employee:

$$£3,541,000/117 = £30,264.96$$

FOULKS LYNCH
PUBLICATIONS

ACTIVITY 31

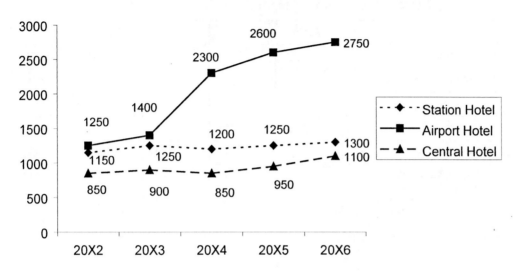

Revenue from room let
20X2–20X6

(b)

MEMORANDUM

To: Hotel Accountant

Form: Accounting Technician

Subject: Trends in Revenue from Rooms Let 20X2–20X6

Date: 17 June 20X5

The graph shows considerably different trends between the Airport Hotel and the other two hotels.

Both the Station and Central Hotels showed a fall in revenue in 2000 with an unspectacular rise in the other years. The rise is hardly significant at the Station Hotel, if marginally more so at the Central Hotel.

The Airport Hotel, on the other hand, has shown a considerable increase over the period, steady rises in 20X3, 20X5 and 20X6 with a huge rise of almost 100% in 20X4. This rise is so marked that it must have been caused by unusual circumstances, perhaps an increase in the size of the hotel.

The most important limitation with the data is that inflation has not been taken into account. Were inflation taken into account the increases would be less, indeed in some cases they may turn into decreases.

ACTIVITY 32

(a)

Super Shops

Shop Performance Ratio Table for the year ended 31 March 20X3

	North	South	East	West	Total
Gross Profit/Sales (%)	27.03	21.36	31.45	31.58	27.86
Net Profit/Sales (%)	2.62	– 1.53	4.52	0.66	2.06
Expense Ratios:					
Wages/Sales (%)	4.93	5.10	8.23	4.39	6.07
Rent/Sales (%)	13.16	11.17	12.34	14.69	12.60
Sundries/Sales (%)	1.70	1.17	2.74	1.97	1.98
Central Costs/Sales (%)	4.62	5.46	3.63	9.87	5.15

REPORT

To: Mr Shah

From: A Technician

Subject: Shop Performance year ended 31 March 20X3

Date: 16 June 20X3

The purpose of this report is to compare the performance of the shops: North, South, East and West, in terms of profitability and cost control. The report is based on the Profit and Loss Account and Performance Ratios for the year ended 31 March 20X3.

Gross Profit/Sales Ratio

The business average is 27.86%. Two shops, East and West, had ratios above the business' average, whereas North was very slightly below the average and South significantly below the average. It may be that the South manager has been reducing the price at which he/she has been selling goods more than the other managers in an effort to improve sales. Otherwise there might have been a change in sales mix towards products with a lower margin or an increase in pilferage within the shop.

Wages/Sales Ratio

There is quite a significant difference between the figure for East and the figures for the other three shops. Whilst East is above average, the other shops are below average. Since the employment of shop assistants appears to be the responsibility of the shop managers then there may be a case for the manager of East reducing the number of staff he/she employs and thereby improving the overall profitability of the business.

Rent/Sales Ratio

West seems to be somewhat above average and South somewhat below, the other two shops being close to the average. Clearly the managers have no control over rent, it being the responsibility of the owner to decide the location of the shops.

FOULKS LYNCH
PUBLICATIONS

Sundries/Sales Ratio

East is above average with South below average and the other two shops close to average. Again, where the manager has the responsibility to spend money, the manager of East appears to be the most profligate.

Central Costs/Sales Ratio

West is well above average and East well below average with the others close to average, but the figures here are controlled by company policy. To divide the central costs equally between the four shops is extremely arbitrary. To judge the performance of the shops fairly the distribution of the central costs between shops should be made according to their usage of the central resources, or else the figures should be omitted from the profit statements for individual shops.

Overall Profitability

On the figures given, East is the most profitable shop in terms of both net profit and net profit as a % of sales, and South makes a loss. However, the results are skewed by the method whereby the central costs are split between the shops. If the central costs are omitted then overall profits can be shown as follows:

	Profit (excluding central costs)	Profit as % of sales
North	£70,500	7.25
South	£32,400	3.93
East	£101,000	8.15
West	£48,000	10.53
Total	£251,900	7.21

These figures now show South is profitable, i.e., it makes a contribution to profit and central costs. It also shows that West is the best performing shop and that both North and East are above average. However, these figures still include rent and by excluding rent we would be better able to judge the performance of the managers in managing the resources over which they have control.

Limitations of the analysis

The data is limited in two respects:

- We are using data for one year only. To judge a shop's performance on one year's figures is rather unfair. It would be better to reveal trends in profitability over time.

- There are no figures for other similar businesses or industry standard figures or budget figures with which to make comparisons. Whilst we can say that the business is profitable and that the performance of shop X is better than that of shop Y, we cannot say that the performance is good or bad in relation to other businesses or the planned budget.

INTRODUCTION TO VAT – SUPPLIES AND REGISTRATION

ACTIVITY 33

		£
(a)	Net price	216.00
	VAT £216 × 17.5%	37.80
	Gross price	253.80
(b)	Net price	5,926.00
	VAT £5,926 × 17.5%	1,037.05
	Gross price	6,963.05
(c)	Net price	11,144.00
	VAT £11,144 × 17.5%	1,950.20
	Gross price	13,094.20

ACTIVITY 34

		£
(a)	Gross price	715.81
	VAT £715.81 × 7/47	106.61
	Net price	609.20

(Check £609.20 × 17.5% = £106.61)

		£
(b)	Gross price	1,292.50
	VAT £1,292.50 × 7/47	192.50
	Net price	1,100.00

(Check £1,100 × 17.5% = £192.50)

		£
(c)	Gross price	7,336.23
	VAT £7,336.23 × 7/47	1,092.63
	Net price	6,243.60

(Check £6,243.60 × 17.5% = £1,092.63)

ACTIVITY 35

Su Chin

	£
Purchase price	1,000
VAT (£1,000 × 17.5%)	175
	——
Total price	1,175
	——
Selling price	3,000
VAT (£3,000 × 17.5%)	525
	——
Total price	3,525
	——
Therefore:	
Input VAT	175
Output VAT	525
	——
VAT due to Customs & Excise	350
	——

This £350 is the VAT at 17.5% on the value added by Su Chin, (£3,000 - £1,000) × 17.5%.

Jake

	£
Purchase price	3,000
VAT (£3,000 × 17.5%)	525
	——
Total price	3,525
	——
Selling price	6,000
VAT (£6,000 × 17.5%)	1,050
	——
Total price	7,050
	——
Therefore:	
Input VAT	525
Output VAT	1,050
	——
VAT due to Customs & Excise	525
	——

This £525 is the VAT at 17.5% on the value added by Jake, (£6,000 – £3,000) × 17.5%.

Consumer

	£
Purchase price	6,000
VAT (£6,000 × 17.5%)	1,050
	———
Total price	7,050
	———

As the consumer does not resell the cello then there is no output tax on which to set off the input tax of £1,050 that has been incurred. The consumer must bear the full cost of the VAT.

The VAT of £1,050 borne by the consumer has been accounted for to HM Customs & Excise in stages, as follows:

	Net Price £	Tax £
By the wood producer:		
Wood	1,000	175
By Su Chin		
Value added	2,000	350
	———	———
	3,000	525
By Jake		
Value added	3,000	525
	———	———
	6,000	1,050
	———	———

ACTIVITY 36

	£
VAT on purchase (£1,762.50 × 17.5/117.5)	262.50
VAT on sale (£2,000 × 17.5%)	350.00
	———
VAT paid to Customs & Excise	87.50
	———

ACTIVITY 37

Exempt supplies are outside the scope of VAT, for example insurance services. A zero-rated supply is taxable but at a rate of 0%, for example books and newspapers.

ACTIVITY 38

(a)   The time at which they are collected, delivered or made available to the customer.

(b)   The date on which all the work is complete.

VAT INVOICES, VAT PERIODS, RECORDS REQUIRED

ACTIVITY 39

(a)   The invoice has no identifying number.

(b)   The invoice does not show the VAT registration number of XYZ Ltd.

(c)   There is no description of the goods.

(d)   The VAT has been incorrectly calculated. A maximum cash discount of 3% is offered for payment within 10 days therefore the VAT should be calculated on £2,160 net of this cash discount whether or not it is taken. The correct amount of VAT is therefore $17.5\% \times £2,160.00 - (3\% \times £2,160.00) = £366.66$.

ACTIVITY 40

(a)   The invoice does not show the time of supply.

(b)   The invoice does not describe the goods or services.

(c)   The invoice has not been completed to show the rate of VAT.

ACTIVITY 41

	Net	VAT @ 17.5%	Gross
	£	£	£
(a)	200.00	35.00	235.00
(b)	1,300.00	227.50	1,527.50
(c)	4,444.00	777.70	5,221.70

ACTIVITY 42

	Gross	VAT @ 7/47	Net
	£	£	£
(a)	117.03	17.43	99.60
(b)	1,238.45	184.45	1,054.00
(c)	7,153.87	1,065.47	6,088.40

ACTIVITY 43

	£
Net price of goods	1,000.00
VAT ((£1,000 – £30) × 17.5%)	169.75
	————
	1,169.75
	————

The VAT is calculated on the net price of the goods assuming that the highest cash discount offered is taken up. The VAT does not alter even if the cash discount is not taken up.

ACTIVITY 44

The VAT charged on the supplies is calculated on the assumption that the 5% cash discount will be taken. By rounding each line on the invoice to the nearest 0.5p the VAT charged is:

	Amount liable to VAT	VAT @ 17.5%
	£	£
5 crates 5 × £10.05 = £50.25 less 5%	47.74	8.355
8 tubs 8 × £13.25 = £106 less 5%	100.70	17.620
6 barrels 6 × £15.15= £90.90 less 5%	86.35	15.110
		————
		41.085
		————
Total VAT charged on the invoice (rounding down)		£41.08

ACTIVITY 45

(a) Giles should apply to have prescribed accounting periods ending 31 March, 30 June, 30 September and 31 December.

(b) Giles should apply to have monthly prescribed accounting periods.

ACTIVITY 46

He must complete and send a return no later than 28 February 20X9. Payments are made as follows:

		£
Year to 31 December 20X8		
Quarterly payments commencing 30 April 20X8	3 @ £720	2,160
Final payment no later than 28 February 20X9	£(3,820 – 2,160)	1,660
		———
		3,820
		———
Year to 31 December 20X9		
Quarterly payments commencing 30 April 20X9		
3 @ £(3,820 × 20%) = 3 @ £764		2,292
		———

ACTIVITY 47

Larry's records are not adequate for the following reasons:

(a)   The records of outputs should:

    (i)   be in the same order as the invoices i.e. in order of issue not payment, and

    (ii)   include the VAT exclusive amount of the supplies.

(b)   The invoices for supplies received should be filed in such a way that they can easily be referred to.

(c)   The records of inputs should:

    (i)   be in such an order as is possible to easily locate the supporting invoice; and

    (ii)   include the VAT exclusive amount of the inputs.

(d)   The VAT account must be kept up to date for each VAT period.

COMPLETING THE VAT RETURN

ACTIVITY 48

(a) **Invoice No 001**

The VAT shown on the invoice is too low. Michael should either:

(i)	account for VAT of $\frac{7}{47} \times £2,300 =$	£342.55
	and adjust the net output to	£1,957.45
	or	
(ii)	issue an additional invoice for	£50.00
	account for VAT of	£350.00
	leaving the net output at	£2,000.00

(b) **Invoice No 002**

The VAT shown on the invoice is too high. Michael should either:

(i)	account for VAT of	£400.00
	and leave the net output at	£2,000.00
	or	
(ii)	issue a credit note for	£50.00
	account for VAT of	£350.00
	leaving the net output at	£2,000.00

ACTIVITY 49

		£	£
(a)	**Outputs**		
	Sales day book		
	Mar sales	23,000	
	Apr sales	21,000	
	May sales	22,000	
	Furniture	2,000	
		———	68,000
	Cash receipts book		
	Mar sales	2,000	
	Apr sales	1,000	
	May sales	2,000	
		———	5,000
	Total outputs		73,000

(b)   **Output tax**

	£	£
Sales day book		
Mar	4,025	
Apr	3,675	
May	4,200	
	———	
		11,900
Cash receipts book		
Mar	350	
Apr	175	
May	350	
	———	
		875
Total output tax		12,775

(c)   **Inputs**

	£	£
Purchases day book		
Mar purchases	16,000	
expenses	2,000	
Apr purchases	14,000	
expenses	3,000	
May purchases	14,000	
expenses	2,000	
	———	
		51,000
Cash payments book		
Mar purchases	1,600	
Apr purchases	2,400	
May purchases	2,000	
	———	
		6,000
Total inputs		57,000

(d)   **Input tax**

	£	£
Purchases day book		
Mar	3,150	
Apr	2,975	
May	2,800	
	———	
		8,925
Cash payments book		
Mar	280	
Apr	420	
May	350	
	———	
		1,050
Total input tax		9,975

ACTIVITY 50

Summary of outputs

	Gross £	VAT £	Net £	Discount £
1	2,332.50	332.50	2,000	100
2	4,198.50	598.50	3,600	180
3	4,665.00	665.00	4,000	200
4	6,997.50	997.50	6,000	300
5	11,662.50	1,662.50	10,000	500
	29,856.00	4,256.00	25,600	1,280

Summary of inputs

	Gross £	VAT £	Net £
Less detailed	1,880.00	280.00	1,600
Invoice	11,750.00	1,750.00	10,000
	13,630.00	2,030.00	11,600

FOULKS LYNCH
PUBLICATIONS

Value Added Tax Return
For the period
to

HM Customs and Excise

For Official Use

Registration number

Period

You could be liable to a financial penalty if your completed return and all the VAT payable are not received by the due date.

Due date:

For official use D O R only	

Fold Here

Before you fill in this form please read the notes on the back and the VAT leaflet *"Filling in your VAT return"*. Fill all boxes clearly in ink, and write 'none' where necessary. Don't put a dash or leave any box blank. If there are no pence write "00" in the pence column. Do **not** enter more than one amount in any box.

For official use			£	p
VAT due in this period on **sales** and other outputs	**1**		4,256	00
VAT due in this period on **acquisitions** from other **EC Member States**	**2**		NONE	
Total VAT due (**the sum of boxes 1 and 2**)	**3**		4,256	00
VAT reclaimed in this period on **purchases** and other inputs (including acquisitions from the EC)	**4**		2,030	00
Net VAT to be paid to Customs or reclaimed by you (**Difference between boxes 3 and 4**)	**5**		2,226	00
Total value of **sales** and all other outputs excluding any VAT. **Include your box 8 figure**	**6**		25,600	00
Total value of **purchases** and all other inputs excluding any VAT. **Include your box 9 figure**	**7**		11,600	00
Total value of **all supplies** of goods and related services, excluding any VAT, to other **EC Member States**	**8**		NONE	00
Total value of all **acquisitions** of goods and related services, excluding any VAT, from other **EC Member States**	**9**		NONE	00

If you are enclosing a payment please tick this box	DECLARATION: You, or someone on your behalf, must sign below.

I, ... declare that the
(Full name of signatory in BLOCK LETTERS)
information given above is true and complete.

Signature .... Date ....
A false declaration can result in prosecution

SPECIAL CASES (VAT)

ACTIVITY 51

(a) **Outputs**

Date	VAT £	Net £
3.6.X7	245	1,400
21.6.X7	175	1,000
11.7.X7	350	2,000
23.8.X7	280	1,600
29.8.X7	385	2,200
	1,435	8,200

(b) **Inputs**

Date	VAT £	Net £
29.6.X7	105	600
29.6.X7	140	800
30.7.X7	175	1,000
30.7.X7	525	3,000
29.8.X7	105	600
	1,050	6,000

ACTIVITY 52

Bad debt relief will be given for £875 as follows:

	Gross £	VAT £
21.1.X4	3,000	
12.2.X4	2,350	350
11.3.X4	3,525	525
		875

Bad debt relief of £350 can be claimed on 12 September 20X4 and £525 on 11 October 20X4, so the relief should be claimed as input tax on the returns for the quarters ended 30 September 20X4 and 31 December 20X4.

VAT ADMINISTRATION

ACTIVITY 53

Delivery charges (postage and packing) etc

If, when you supply goods, you make an arrangement to deliver or post them for an extra charge, the extra charge is for the supply of a separate delivery service. If you send goods by post, the charge made to you by the Post Office is exempt, but your charge to your customer is taxable even if it is exactly equal to the charge made to you by the Post Office. Your supply of delivery services is standard-rated if the goods are sent to an address in the UK and zero-rated if they are sent elsewhere.

However, if the terms of your agreement with your customer for the supply of the goods requires you to deliver or post them to him, there is no separate supply of delivery or postage. This applies even if you show a separate charge. This means that you make a single supply of delivered goods and if the supply of the goods is zero-rated then the zero rating also covers the delivery or postage. This applies to most mail order transactions, but not if a delivery service is available at an extra charge for customers who request it.

Applying this guidance to Jack's case, the solution is:

(a) If the arrangement to post the goods is a one-off arrangement, then the charge for postage and packing is standard rated.

(b) If delivery is part of Jack's normal terms of sale, the charge will be zero rated as there will be a single supply of goods and delivery.

ACTIVITY 54

(a) The changes should be notified by 3 March 20X8.

R 'N R Services
High Street
Anytown HB33 9LN

28 February 20X8

HM Customs and Excise
Anytown Business Park
Whereshire

Dear Sir or Madam

VAT Registration No 452 6870 01

Please be advised that with effect from 1 February 20X8, a new partner, Naomi Fenn, was admitted to our partnership. At the same time we changed our trading name from R & R Services to R 'N R Services.

Yours faithfully,

Richard Brooks

Robert Brooks

(Partners)

FOULKS LYNCH
PUBLICATIONS

ANSWERS TO SPECIMEN SIMULATION

SIMULATION 1

TASK 1

Sales to external customers

Manufacturing and Sales divisions combined

	Monthly totals £000	Cumulative total for the year £000
20X1/20X2		
April	384	384
May	271	655
June	222	877
July	309	1,186
August	346	1,532
September	262	1,794
October	240	2,034
November	329	2,363
December	279	2,642
January	277	2,919
February	244	3,163
March	385	3,548
20X2/20X3		
April	381	381
May	242	623
June	237	860
July	339	1,199
August	330	1,529
September	299	1,828
October	231	2,059
November	372	2,431

December	355	2,786
January	310	3,096
February	272	3,368
March	291	3,659

TASK 2

Cumulative external sales 20X1/20X2 and 20X2/20X3

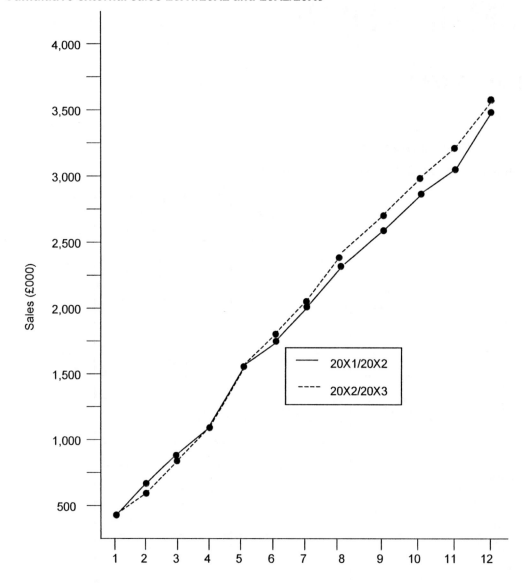

TASK 3

Indexed sales to external customers

Manufacturing and Sales divisions combined

	Unadjusted totals £000	Index factor	Indexed totals £000
20X2/20X3			
April	381	131.0/123.8	403
May	242	131.0/124.4	255
June	237	131.0/124.9	249
July	339	131.0/125.7	353
August	330	131.0/126.3	342
September	299	131.0/127.0	308
October	231	131.0/127.5	237
November	372	131.0/128.1	380
December	355	131.0/128.9	361
January	310	131.0/129.6	313
February	272	131.0/130.2	274
March	291	131.0/131.0	291

Notes

1. In the first column, insert the monthly totals of external sales calculated in Task 1.

2. In the second column, insert the index factor required to convert to March 20X3 values.

Note: The index for March 20X3 is 131.0. To convert figures in other months to March 20X3 values, we have to multiply by a factor 131.0/month's index.

3. In the third column, calculate the monthly sales in March 20X3 terms (to the nearest £1,000).

TASK 4

LOAN APPLICATION (extract)

Name of applicant company	Homer Limited
Latest year for which accounting information is available	Year ended 31 March 20X3
Total sales revenue	
In latest year for which accounts are available	£ 3,659,000
In previous year	£ 3,548,000
Percentage change (+/-)	+3.13%
Net profit after all expenses, before taxation	
In latest year for which accounts are available	£ 310,000
In previous year	£ 278,000
Percentage change (+/-)	+11.51%
Gross profit margin (%)	40.17%
Net profit margin (%)	8.47%
Return on capital employed (%)	4.70%

Notes

1. In the case of a company with a divisional structure, all figures should refer to the results of the company as a whole, not to individual divisions within the company.

2. Unless otherwise stated, all questions relate to the latest year for which accounting information is available.

3. Figures should be actual historical values, with no indexing for inflation.

4. Return on capital employed is defined as net profit for the year before taxation, divided by total capital employed.

Workings

	Revenue	Net profit
	£000	£000
Most recent year	3,659	310
Previous year	3,548	278
Increase	+111	+32
% change	$\left(\frac{111}{3,659}\right) \times 100\%$	$\left(\frac{32}{310}\right) \times 100\%$
	= + 3.13%	= + 11.51%

FOULKS LYNCH
PUBLICATIONS

Gross profit margin	=	$\left(\dfrac{1{,}470}{3{,}659}\right) \times 100\%$
	=	40.17%
Net profit margin	=	$\left(\dfrac{310}{3{,}659}\right) \times 100\%$
	=	8.47%
Return on capital employed	=	Net profit/capital employed
	=	$\left(\dfrac{310}{6{,}590}\right) \times 100\%$
	=	4.70%

MEMO

To:	Sonia Liesl
From:	Amir Pindhi
Subject:	Loan application form
Date:	14 April 20X3

I attach the completed loan application form for your approval before its submission to the bank.

If you need any further information please let me know.

TASK 5

MEMO

To: Sonia Liesl

From: Amir Pindhi

Subject: Statistics for the year ended 31 March 20X3

Date: 14 April 20X3

I have calculated the statistics you requested, for the year ended 31 March 20X3.

1.   The **gross profit percentage** is 40.17%. This has fallen from 43.15% the previous year. This could be due to an increase in production costs (see point 3 below)

2.   The **net profit percentage** is 8.47%. This has risen from 7.84% the previous year, in spite of the fall in gross profit percentage. This is probably due to good control of overhead costs.

3.   The **production cost per unit** is £11.01. This has risen from £10.83 in the previous year, possibly because of higher material costs.

4.   The **value of sales earned per employee** is £25,587.41. This has fallen from £26,018.13 the previous year. The percentage increase in the number of employees must have been higher than the 3.13% increase in sales revenue.

Workings:

Production cost per unit $= \dfrac{£2,190,000}{199,000}$

                                          $= $ £11.01

Value of sales earned per employee $= \dfrac{£3,659,000}{143}$

                                          $= $ £25,587.41

TASK 6

HM Customs and Excise

Value Added Tax Return
For the period
01–01–X3 **to** 31–03–X3

For Official Use

Registration number	Period
625 7816 29	03 X3

You could be liable to a financial penalty if your completed return and all the VAT payable are not received by the due date.

Due date: 30.04.X3

┌   ┐

HOMER LIMITED
SESTOS DRIVE
PANTILE TRADING ESTATE
CV32 1AW

└   ┘

For official use DOR only	

Fold | Here

Before you fill in this form please read the notes on the back and the VAT leaflet *"Filling in your VAT return"*. Fill all boxes clearly in ink, and write 'none' where necessary. Don't put a dash or leave any box blank. If there are no pence write "00" in the pence column. Do **not** enter more than one amount in any box.

For official use				£	p
	VAT due in this period on **sales** and other outputs	**1**		139,618	95
	VAT due in this period on **acquisitions** from other **EC Member States**	**2**		NONE	
	Total VAT due (**the sum of boxes 1 and 2**)	**3**		139,618	95
	VAT reclaimed in this period on **purchases** and other inputs (including acquisitions from the EC)	**4**		91,197	54
	Net VAT to be paid to Customs or reclaimed by you (**Difference between boxes 3 and 4**)	**5**		48,421	41
	Total value of **sales** and all other outputs excluding any VAT. **Include your box 8 figure**	**6**		873,012	00
	Total value of **purchases** and all other inputs excluding any VAT. **Include your box 9 figure**	**7**		520,568	00
	Total value of **all supplies** of goods and related services, excluding any VAT, to other **EC Member States**	**8**		75,1890	00
	Total value of all **acquisitions** of goods and related services, excluding any VAT, from other **EC Member States**	**9**		NONE	00

If you are enclosing a payment please tick this box	DECLARATION: You, or someone on your behalf, must sign below.
	I, ... *SONIA LIESL* .... declare that the (Full name of signatory in BLOCK LETTERS) information given above is true and complete. Signature .... Date .... **A false declaration can result in prosecution**

Note The figure in box 4 is the VAT on purchases/expenses (91,099.54) plus VAT reclaimed on the bad debt ($658 \times 7/47 = 98$)

TASK 7

HOMER LIMITED
Sestos Drive, Pantile Trading Estate CV32 1AW
Telephone: 02467 881235

14 April 20X3

H M Customs and Excise
Bell House
33 Lambert Road
Coventry
CV12 8TR

Dear Sir/Madam

This company is considering whether to of import raw materials from a Far Eastern
supplier. We are unsure of the VAT implications of doing this.

I should be grateful if you would send me a copy of any relevant publication dealing with
VAT on imports.

Yours faithfully

Sonia Liesl
ACCOUNTANT

Registered office: Sestos Drive, Pantile Trading Estate CV32 1AW
Registered in England, number 2007814

TASK 8

MEMO

To:	Sonia Liesl
From:	Amir Pindhi
Subject:	VAT on imports
Date:	14 April 20X3

I enclose a draft letter to the local VAT office requesting a copy of any publication on this
topic.

Briefly, the rule is that if we import goods from a non-EC country we have to pay VAT on
import at the standard rate. It will normally be possible to reclaim this as recoverable VAT.

It may be possible to arrange the imports through an appropriate agent who is approved for
duty deferment. If so, we can then defer the payment.

ANSWERS TO PRACTICE SIMULATION 1

TASK 1

Engineering Supplies Limited

This is a valid VAT-only invoice. It should be processed as a March input and the VAT should be reclaimed in the quarter January to March 20X2.

Alpha Stationery

This is a valid VAT invoice of the less detailed kind. It should be processed as a March input and the VAT should be reclaimed in the quarter January to March 20X2.

Jamieson & Co

This is merely a proforma invoice. The service provided by Jamieson & Co cannot be regarded as an input until a valid invoice is received. The VAT should not be reclaimed at this stage.

TASK 2

Value Added Tax Return
For the period
01-01-X2 **to** 31-03-X2

HM Customs and Excise

For Official Use

Registration number	Period
578 4060 19	03 X2

081 578 4060 19 100 03 98 Q35192
MR SHERRY TEDDINGHAM
HODDLE LIMITED
22 FORMGUARD STREET
PEXLEY
PX6 2QW

You could be liable to a financial penalty if your completed return and all the VAT payable are not received by the due date.

Due date: 30.04.X2

For official use D O R only	

Fold Here

Before you fill in this form please read the notes on the back and the VAT leaflet *"Filling in your VAT return"*. Fill all boxes clearly in ink, and write 'none' where necessary. Don't put a dash or leave any box blank. If there are no pence write "00" in the pence column. Do **not** enter more than one amount in any box.

For official use			£	p
	VAT due in this period on **sales** and other outputs	**1**	7,740	12
	VAT due in this period on **acquisitions** from other **EC Member States**	**2**	NONE	
	Total VAT due (**the sum of boxes 1 and 2**)	**3**	7,740	12
	VAT reclaimed in this period on **purchases** and other inputs (including acquisitions from the EC)	**4**	13,477	96
	Net VAT to be paid to Customs or reclaimed by you (**Difference between boxes 3 and 4)**	**5**	5,737	84
	Total value of **sales** and all other outputs excluding any VAT. **Include your box 8 figure**	**6**	120,606	00
	Total value of **purchases** and all other inputs excluding any VAT. **Include your box 9 figure**	**7**	80,727	00
	Total value of **all supplies** of goods and related services, excluding any VAT, to other **EC Member States**	**8**	10,870	00
	Total value of all **acquisitions** of goods and related services, excluding any VAT, from other **EC Member States**	**9**	NONE	00

If you are enclosing a payment please tick this box	DECLARATION: You, or someone on your behalf, must sign below.
	I, ... SHERRY TEDDINGHAM .... declare that the
	(Full name of signatory in BLOCK LETTERS)
	information given above is true and complete.
4	Signature .... Date 9 April 20X2
	A false declaration can result in prosecution

Workings

		£
Box 4	PDB	12,690.53
	Petty cash	244.95
	Bad debt	73.50
	Engineering Supplies invoice	466.77
	Alpha Stationery invoice	2.21
		13,477.96
Box 7	PDB	79,179.67
	Petty cash	1,535.34
	Alpha Stationery invoice	12.63
		80,727.64

TASK 3

HODDLE LIMITED

22 Formguard Street, Pexley PY6 3QW

9 April 20X2

HM Customs & Excise
Brendon House
14 Abbey Street
Pexley PY2 3WR

Dear Sirs

Registration number: 578 4060 19

This company at present accounts for VAT on the basis of invoices raised and received. We are

considering the idea of changing to the cash accounting scheme, and I would be grateful if you

could provide some information on this. Perhaps there is a leaflet setting out details of the scheme?

The particular points of which we are uncertain are as follows:

- What turnover limits apply to the scheme? Are these limits affected by the fact that this company is part of a group consisting of the company itself and its parent company?

- How are bad debts accounted for under the cash accounting scheme?

I would be grateful for any assistance you are able to give on these points, and generally about the workings of the scheme.

Yours faithfully

Sherry Teddingham
ACCOUNTANT

TASK 4

CONSOLIDATED PROFIT AND LOSS ACCOUNT
FOR THE THREE MONTHS ENDED 31 MARCH 20X2

	Kelly £	*Hoddle* £	*Adjustments* £	*Consolidated* £
Sales	295,768	120,607	20,167	396,208
Opening stock	28,341	14,638		42,979
Purchases	136,095	50,908	18,271	168,732
	164,436	65,546		211,711
Closing stock	31,207	16,052	1,896	49,155
Cost of sales	133,229	49,494*		162,556
Gross profit	162,539	71,113		233,652
Wages and salaries	47,918	18,014		65,932
Distribution expenses	28,341	13,212		41,553
Administration expenses	30,189	11,676		41,865
Stationery	2,541	544*		3,085
Travel	2,001	267		2,268
Office expenses	3,908	737		4,645
Interest payable	12,017			12,017
Other expenses	11,765	3,384		15,149
	138,680	47,834		186,514
Net profit for the period	23,859	23,279		47,138

Workings

HODDLE'S COST OF SALES, JAN - MAR 20X2

	£
Opening stock	14,638.00
Purchases	50,908.21
	65,546.21
Closing stock	16,052.00
Cost of sales	49,494.21

Hoddle's stationery costs, Jan - Mar 20X2

	£
Petty cash book	531.55
Alpha Stationery invoice	12.63
	544.18

*Workings sheet for tasks 5 & 6**

QUARTERLY CONSOLIDATED PROFIT AND LOSS ACCOUNTS
FOR THE YEAR ENDED 31 MARCH 20X2

	1 Apr 20X1 30 Jun 20X1 £	1 Jul 20X1 30 Sep 20X1 £	1 Oct 20X1 31 Dec 20X1 £	1 Jan 20X2 31 Mar 20X2 £	1 Apr 20X1 31 Mar 20X2 £
Sales	325,719	275,230	306,321	396,208	1,303,478
Cost of sales	134,861	109,421	121,358	162,556	528,196
Gross profit	190,858	165,809	184,963	233,652	775,282
Wages and salaries	63,314	61,167	64,412	65,932	254,825
Distribution expenses	34,217	30,135	31,221	41,553	137,126
Administration expenses	34,765	33,012	36,415	41,865	146,057
Stationery	2,981	2,671	3,008	3,085	11,745
Travel	1,975	1,876	2,413	2,268	8,532
Office expenses	4,412	4,713	3,083	4,645	16,853
Interest payable	12,913	12,714	12,432	12,017	50,076
Other expenses	10,891	16,421	15,431	15,149	57,982
	165,558	162,709	168,415	186,514	683,196
Net profit for the period	25,300	3,100	16,548	47,138	92,086

*   Completing this schedule is just one possible way of deriving the figures needed to carry out the tasks and not all students will necessarily fill it in.

TASK 5

REPORT

To: Sherry Teddingham
From: Sol Bellcamp
Subject: Report on group results for the year ended 31 March 20X2
Date: 9 April 20X2

Introduction

This report contains the usual information on group results for the year, plus the additional information requested in your memo to me of 2 April 20X2.

Key ratios

Gross profit margin = £775,282 ÷ £1,303,478 = 59.5%

Net profit margin = £92,086 ÷ £1,303,478 = 7.1%

Return on shareholders' capital employed = £92,086 ÷ £1,034,708 = 8.9%

Sales revenue by quarter

Quarter	Unindexed		Indexed (base period = first quarter 20X0/20X1)
	£		£
Apr – Jun 20X1	325,719	(× 231.8/239.3)	315,511
Jul – Sep 20X1	275,230	(× 231.8/241.5)	264,175
Oct – Dec 20X1	306,321	(× 231.8/244.0)	291,005
Jan – Mar 20X2	396,208	(× 231.8/241.8)	379,822

Pie chart showing sales by quarter

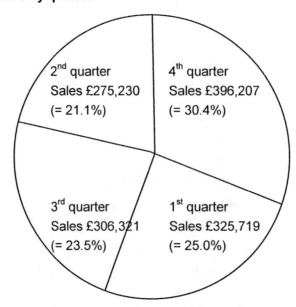

TASK 6

INTERFIRM COMPARISON DATA (extracts)

Name of company ....*Kelly Limited and Subsidiary*...........

Year ended ....*31 March 20X2*................................

Data

	£	% of sales	Industry best	Industry average
Sales	1,303,478			
Gross profit	775,282	59.5%	62.1%	57.3%
Net profit	92,086	7.1%	10.4%	5.8%
Fixed assets	1,229,348			
Current assets	325,703			
Current liabilities	148,271			
Return on capital employed		10.1%	10.3%	9.0%

TASK 7

MEMO
To: Sherry Teddingham **From:** Sol Bellcamp **Subject:** Interfirm comparison data **Date:** 9 April 20X2 I enclose the completed interfirm comparison data for the year ended 31 March 20X2. Please let me know if you disagree with anything in it; otherwise, it is ready for despatch subject to your authorisation.

ANSWERS TO PRACTICE SIMULATION 2

TASK 1

The condition and performance ratios are presented in the pro forma company analysis sheets as follows:

Liquidity/Cashflow indicators

Financial year	20X0	20X1	20X2
Current ratio: [Current assets: Current liabilities]	1.61:1	2.02:1	2.54:1
Acid test ratio: [Current assets – Stocks: Current liabilities]	1.01:1	1.20:1	1.45:1
Cash ratio: [Cash: Current liabilities]	0.35 : 1	0.38 : 1	0.39 : 1

Performance indicators

Financial year	20X0	20X1	20X2
Return on capital employed (ROCE) [Net profit/Shareholders' investment × 100 (%)]	4.71%	5.15%	10.44%
Net profit margin [Net profit/Sales × 100 (%)]	2.75%	3.31%	6.62%
Asset efficiency/Turnover [Sales/Net total assets]	1.71 times	1.56 times	1.58 times
Gross profit margin [Gross profit/Sales × 100 (%)]	46.28%	44.44%	45.28%
Expense: Sales ratios			
Admin. expenses: Sales	32.09%	31.30%	29.63%
Distribution costs: Sales	10.84%	10.12%	10.07%
Interest costs: Sales	1.69%	1.65%	2.76%

[All measured as % figures]			
Fixed asset efficiency/Turnover			
[Sales/Fixed assets]	2.24 times	2.23 times	2.24 times
Stock turnover			
[Cost of sales: Average stock]	3.11	3.10	2.82
Debtor turnover			
[Sales: Debtors]	5.16	5.16	5.03
Debtor payment period			
[Debtors/Sales × 365]	70.7 days	70.7 days	72.6 days
Creditor turnover			
[Purchases: Creditors]	2.28	3.03	4.0
Creditor payment period			
[Creditors/Purchases × 365]	160.1 days	120.6 days	91.3 days

Workings

All figures are directly worked using figures for the balances suggested in the pro forma document.

Note that:

– Shareholders' investment for ROCE is measured as capital plus retained profits at the end of each year. Thus 20X0 ROCE is measured as 11.1 ÷ 235.7 = 4.71% and so forth for later years.

– Net profit is taken as the net profit referred to in the profit and loss statements – ie, before taxation.

– Stock turnover is computed as suggested. For 20X0 we have:

> Cost of sales = £216,600

> Average stock = (£68,300 + £71,000) ÷ 2 = £69,650

> Thus stock turnover = £216,600 ÷ £69,650 = 3.11

Similar calculations apply for other years.

– As specific debtor figures are not given for each year, the figure taken for debtor calculations is that of 'debtors and prepayments' (being the closest approximation to debtor figures).

– Trade creditor figures have been used to assess creditor turnover and creditor periods.

Tutorial note: the figures to use in the ratios have been quite clearly specified in the pro forma. However, any reasonable variations around the points made in the above notes would be accepted.

TASK 2

Suggested responses to Jeff's comments are as follows

1. The inflation indices given in my earlier note indicate an inflation rate of 6% annually over 20X1 and 20X2.

   Comment

   Yes they do. The indices reflect a year-on-year 6% increase, ie:

   – For 20X0/X1, the index increase is $(118.72 - 112.00) \div 112.00 = 0.06$ or 6%

   – For 20X1/X2, the index increase is $(125.84 - 118.72) \div 118.72 = 0.06$ or 6%

2. The sales position is not healthy. Sales revenues have been growing and sales prices have been increasing roughly in line with inflation rates. However, inflation-adjusted 20X2 and 20X3 sales revenue figures to 20X1 price levels indicate that sales volumes have been falling.

   Comment

   Yes, this is true; note that:

   – 20X0 sales value is £403,200

   – 20X1 sales value adjusted to 20X0 price levels is

   $$£423,000 \times \frac{112.0}{118.72} = £399,057$$

   – 20X2 sales value adjusted to 20X0 price levels is

   $$£442,800 \times \frac{112.0}{125.84} = £394,100$$

   Sales value in real terms and sales volumes are falling.

3. The improved company performance over the three year period is largely a product of highly-effective cost control as indicated by cost of sales: sales and expenses: sales ratios.

   Comment

   All the cost ratios mentioned were calculated in Task 1 excepting cost of sales:sales. This latter ratio is calculated as 53.72%, 55.56% and 54.72% for the three years respectively.

   All expenses:sales ratios (excepting interest cost:sales) have shown improvement over the three-year period. However, cost of sales:sales has shown some deterioration. There seems to be evidence of some control of general expenses/costs but not necessarily of cost of sales.

   The reduction in expenses:sales figures have been responsible for some overall increase in net profit margins which, given increases in sales values, have resulted in good increases in net profits. However, another big contributor appears to have been 'other income' which accounts for £12,400 (£16,800 – £4,400) of the net profit increase of £29,300 – £11,100 = £18,200.

   The statement is partly true. Control of general expenses and 'other income' seems largely responsible for improved performance.

4. The balance sheet figures show outstanding debt liabilities at the end of each year. These figures are not reflective/representative of the average amount of debt outstanding over the whole of each respective year.

Using the figures for the average interest rate charged to us annually and our annual interest charges in the P/L (from the earlier statements), the average amounts of interest-bearing debt over each year have been £37,777, £36,842 and £97,600 respectively.

Comment

This is true. Balance sheet debt (at least as far as discernible from the figures given) has increased from £17,200 (20X0) to £18,600 (20X1) and £45,000 (20X2). Estimates of interest-bearing debt for each year are as follows:

$$- \quad \text{20X0} \quad £6,800 \times \frac{100}{18} = £37,777 \; (= \text{Interest for year} \times \frac{100}{\text{Interest rate}})$$

$$- \quad \text{20X1} \quad £7,000 \times \frac{100}{19} = £36,842$$

$$- \quad \text{20X2} \quad £12,200 \times \frac{100}{12.5} = £97,600$$

These figures agree with those given.

5. The proportion of company profits taken up by taxation has increased over the three-year period.

Comment

True. The figures of taxation ÷ profits before taxation indicate proportionate tax liabilities as follows:

- 20X0 £3,900 ÷ £11,100 = 35.14%

- 20X1 £5,300 ÷ £14,000 = 37.86%

- 20X2 £11,700 ÷ £29,300 = 39.93%

These reflect proportionate increases over the three-year period.

6. Overall total profits have improved over the three-year period and the shareholders have benefited from the improvement. The company is in a healthier state generally.

Comment

Total profits have certainly increased over the period – from £7,200 (20X0) to £8,700 (20X1) and £17,600 (20X2). The shareholders have benefited from increased dividends which have gone up from £3,800 (20X0) to £4,500 (20X1) and £8,800 (20X2). These increases are of more than 6% (the inflation rate) and are therefore real increases. Retained profits have also increased progressively by more than the inflation rate. ROCE (before tax) has also increased (per earlier figures). If ROCE (after tax) figures were calculated, these would be found to be 3.05% (20X0), 3.2% (20X1) and 6.27% (20X2). The shareholders have therefore benefited according to these ROCE measures.

However, the company could not be said to be 'in a healthier state'. Sales volumes (the lifeblood of the company) are falling and the company seems highly dependent on 'other income'.

The position needs careful review. The trading problems must be addressed and resolved if the company is to have a healthy future.

TASK 3

Time series figures are as follows:

TIME SERIES ANALYSIS				
				Figures in £'000
Time periods 20X0	Quarterly figures	4-quarterly moving average figures [Gen. trend]	4-quarterly moving average figures [Centred trend]	Seasonal effects [per quarter]
3 months to 31 March	78.8			
3 months to 30 June	107.2			
		100.80		
3 months to 30 September	85.9		101.525	(15.625)
		102.25		
3 months to 31 December	131.3		103.40	27.9
20X1		104.55		
3 months to 31 March	84.6		105.49	(20.89)
		106.43		
3 months to 30 June	116.4		106.09	10.31
		105.75		
3 months to 30 September	93.4		106.55	(13.15)
		107.35		
3 months to 31 December	128.6		107.75	20.85
20X2		108.15		
3 months to 31 March	91.0		108.75	(17.75)
		109.35		
3 months to 30 June	119.6		110.025	9.575
		110.70		
3 months to 30 September	98.2			
3 months to 31 December	134.0			

Negative figures are shown in brackets.

TASK 4

Time series chart – Sales revenues

Period of analysis – Financial years 20X0 – 20X2

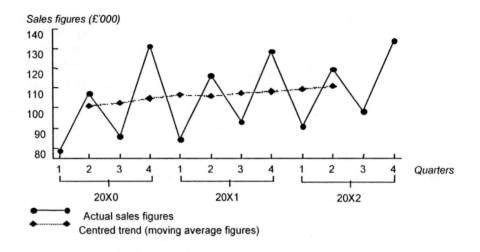

TASK 5

The multiple bar charts might be presented as follows:

Sales revenues – Quarterly results

Period of analysis – Financial years 20X0 – 20X2

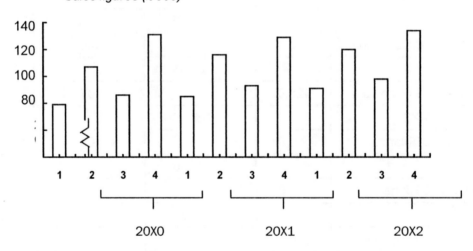

TASK 6

A suitable pie chart might be presented as follows:

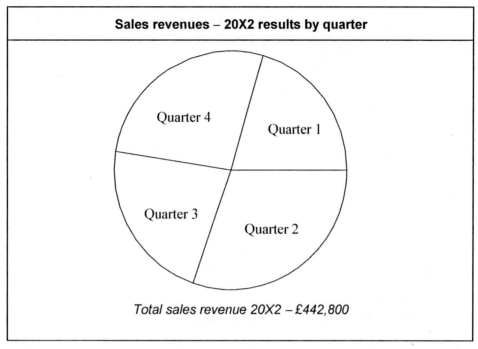

Sales revenues – 20X2 results by quarter

Total sales revenue 20X2 – £442,800

Tutorial note: the chart should be drawn with angles for each sector (measured at the centre of the chart) being:

– For quarter 1: (91.0 ÷ 442.8) × 360 = 74°

– For quarter 2: (119.6 ÷ 442.8) × 360 = 97°

– For quarter 3: (98.2 ÷ 442.8) × 360 = 80°

– For quarter 4: (134.0 ÷ 442.8) × 360 = 109° (All to the nearest degree of angle.)

TASK 7

Analysis is as follows (using the company pro forma analysis sheets):

Edwards Electronics Ltd

Production evaluation

Product: TRISTAR TV

Period: 20X2 (Year)

Production per assembly hour:

205 ÷ 369 = **0.55 units**

Production per machine hour:

205 ÷ 102.5× = **2 units**

Revenue per unit:

£46,550 ÷ 190 = **£245**

TASK 8

The completed return for the Association of Electrical Contractors is as follows:

```
  /‾‾‾‾\        Association of Electrical Contractors
 |  A   |           18, Grafton Way, Herts, HA3 4PF
 |  E   |
 |  C   |
  \____/
```

Annual performance results

ROCE

(PBIT/Shareholders' investment) | 10.44 | Debtor period | 72.6 |

Gross margin on sales | 45.28 | Creditor period

| 91.3 |

Net margin on sales | 6.62 |
(using net profit before tax)

Stock period

| 129.4 |

Asset turnover | 1.58 |
(Sales/Net total assets)   (All periods in days)

Above figure taken from financial statements for the year to/as at... 31 December 20X2....................

Results will be confidentially held and used only to produce general descriptive statistical information for the use of the Association and its members.

Signature...

TASK 9

MEMO

To: Jeff Thompson

From: Accounting Technician

Date:

Subject: Annual return

Please would you check the return that I have completed for the Association of Electrical Contractors? If you are satisfied with it, please sign and return it to me for despatch.

ANSWERS TO PRACTICE SIMULATION 3

TASK 1

	20X1	20X2	20X3	20X4	20X5
Sales value of Axminster (£'000)	94.86	105.84	117.52	127.44	136.53
Sales value of Wilton (£'000)	402.21	474.22	539.58	648.15	736.32
Total sales value (£'000)	497.07	580.06	657.10	775.59	872.85
Value at 19X1 prices (£'000)	497.07	552.57	594.94	677.80	740.27

TASK 2

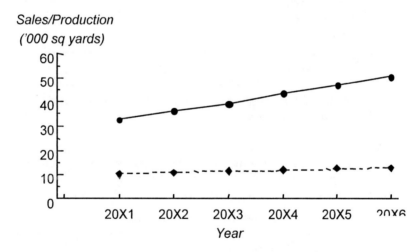

Forecasts for 20X6
Axminster production: 12.8 (i.e., 12,800 sq yds)
Wilton production: 50.6 (i.e., 50,600 sq yds)

TASK 3

MILLS CARPETS LTD

To: The sales director

From: Date:

Subject: Sales and price movements and projections: 20X1 to 20X6

Introduction

This report analyses sales and price variations and trends over the period 20X1 to 20X5 and gives a statistical forecast of sales volume for 20X6.

Summary

There has been a steady increase over the five year period in both sales volume and sales value. The latter is an increase in real terms, allowance having been made for inflation.

Sales prices are, however, rising faster than inflation, which is a trend that needs to be considered carefully.

Findings

1   *Sales volume*

There has been a steady increase in sales for both types of carpet over the five-year period, as summarised in the following table:

Production 20X1 to 20X5

Carpet type	Actual increase ('000 sq yds)	% Increase
Axminster	2.1	20.6
Wilton	14.5	44.3
Combined	16.6	38.7

Production and sales of Wilton carpets has increased at more than twice the rate (44.3%) of Axminster (20.6%).

2   *Prices*

Prices are rising by approximately six index points annually (greater in 20X4 for Wilton). This is greater than the rate of inflation, except for Axminster in 20X2. The overall increases are given below:

Price index for 20X5 (20X1 = 100)

Carpet type	Index for 20X5
Axminster	119
Wilton	127
Index of retail prices (20X1 = 100)	118

From this table, it will be seen that the price of Axminster has risen by one point more and Wilton by nine points more than the IRP over the five-year period.

FOULKS LYNCH
PUBLICATIONS

3   *Sales value*

The sales value is increasing both in actual and real terms, as shown by the following table:

Total sales value – 20X1 to 20X5

	Actual increase (£'000)	*% Increase*
Total sales	375.78	75.6
Deflated sales at 20X1 prices	243.20	48.9

Thus there has been an increase in real terms of 48.9% over the five-year period.

4   *Forecasts for 20X6*

Statistical forecasts of sales volume for 20X6 are:

Axminster   12,800 sq yds

Wilton   50,600 sq yds

As the graphs of production are fairly close to straight lines, the extrapolation to 20X6 should be reliable, provided no new factors occur to change the trends.

Conclusions

The following conclusions can be drawn from this analysis:

–   Demand is steadily increasing and, provided no new factors occur, sales volume for the next year should be budgeted at 12,800 square yards of Axminster and 50,600 square yards of Wilton.

–   Up to the present, the value of sales has been steadily increasing in real terms. However, prices are increasing above the rate of inflation and this will result in increasing sales resistance if the trend is allowed to continue. The causes of this rise in prices should be investigated and the trend halted if the company is to remain competitive.

TASK 4

	20X2	*20X3*	*20X4*
Percentage to turnover:			
Gross profit	51.9	48.9	45.0
Net profit	2.9	2.2	(2.0)
Materials	20.2	17.8	20.0
Labour	15.4	17.8	20.0
Overhead	12.5	15.6	15.0
Administration	25.0	25.6	24.0
Distribution	24.0	21.1	23.0
Percentage change in sales over previous year		(13.5)	11.1
ROCE $\dfrac{\text{Profit before tax}}{\text{Total assets less current liabilities at year end}} \times 100$	5.9%	4.1%	(4.3)%
$\dfrac{\text{Turnover}}{\text{Fixed assets}}$	2.7	2.4	2.9
Current ratio	1.4	1.4	1.4

Quick ratio	0.5	0.5	0.5
Stock turnover $\dfrac{\text{Cost of sales}}{\text{Year-end stock}}$	1.9	1.8	2.1
Raw materials stock turnover $\dfrac{\text{Cost of materials}}{\text{Year-end materials stock}}$	2.1	1.6	2
Debtor collection period	46 days	57 days	55 days

TASK 5

To:　　　　Board of directors

From:

Date:

Subject:　　Franklin plc – Financial analysis

Profitability

The gross profit percentage is about 50% which has declined to 45% in 20X4. The net profit percentage is, however, very low with a loss made in 20X4.

The decline in gross profitability appears mainly to be due to the increase in labour costs which have increased from 15% to 20% of turnover.

Both administration and distribution costs are greater than 20% of turnover. Further detail would be required on the elements making up these costs.

There has been no growth in sales in the period in money terms. In real terms there has been a decline as the general index of retail prices has increased by 9% from 20X2 to 20X4 $\left(\dfrac{230-211}{211}\times 100\right)$.

Return on capital employed has fallen from 6% in 20X2 to a negative return in 20X4. In absolute terms, the 6% ROCE in 20X2 was a poor return for shareholders and the decline is therefore all the more worrying.

The poor ROCE figures are reinforced by the low level of turnover to fixed assets (under 3) and stock turnover (about 2).

In brief, this is not a good performance by the company.

Liquidity

The current and quick ratios have remained constant at 1.4 and 0.5 respectively. These need to be compared with our own ratios to determine whether they are too low or too high. On the face of it, however, their constancy implies sound short-term financial management.

In particular, stock levels have not been allowed to grow despite the lack of sales growth and the low stock turnover ratio. Perhaps this indicates that the management have had no plans for growth.

The debtor collection period has extended from 46 to 55 days and this shows some signs of poor credit control management.

Limitations of analysis

(a)　*Cyclical factors*

　　Many of the ratios are based on successive annual balance sheets at 31 December. The manner in which the assets have been employed in the business at this date may not be representative of the normal level of activity in the business.

Thus stock levels and debtors, for example, may be at a low point at the financial year-end.

(b)   *Lack of detail*

The published accounts contain summary information in many cases. There is insufficient detail on the elements making up an aggregate figure.

(c)   *Accounting policies*

Accounting policies should be consistently applied by the same company but these may be different to ours, making inter-firm comparison difficult.

(d)   *Timeliness of information*

The data is past information from published accounts. The latest information is thus already over a year out of date and may not reflect current circumstances.

ANSWERS TO PRACTICE SIMULATION 4

TASK 1 – VAT RETURN

Value Added Tax Return
For the period
to

HM Customs and Excise

Before you fill in this form please read the notes on the back and the VAT leaflet *"Filling in your VAT return"*. Fill all boxes clearly in ink, and write 'none' where necessary. Don't put a dash or leave any box blank. If there are no pence write "00" in the pence column. Do **not** enter more than one amount in any box.

For official use				£	p
VAT due in this period on **sales** and other outputs	1	(W1)		5,985	74
VAT due in this period on **acquisitions** from other **EC Member States**	2			NONE	
Total VAT due (**the sum of boxes 1 and 2**)	3			5,985	
VAT reclaimed in this period on **purchases** and other inputs (including acquisitions from the EC)	4	(W2)		4,485	16
Net VAT to be paid to Customs or reclaimed by you (**Difference between boxes 3 and 4**)	5	(W3)		1,500	58
Total value of **sales** and all other outputs excluding any VAT. **Include your box 8 figure**	6	(Note 3)		18,775	00
Total value of **purchases** and all other inputs excluding any VAT. **Include your box 9 figure**	7	(Note 5)		9,811	00
Total value of **all supplies** of goods and related services, excluding any VAT, to other **EC Member States**	8			NONE	00
Total value of all **acquisitions** of goods and related services, excluding any VAT, from other **EC Member States**	9			NONE	00

If you are enclosing a payment please tick this box	DECLARATION: You, or someone on your behalf, must sign below. I, ... declare that the (Full name of signatory in BLOCK LETTERS) information given above is true and complete. Signature .... Date .... **A false declaration can result in prosecution**

Workings

(1)   3,285.74 (Note 3) + 2,700.00 = £5,985.74

(2)   1,693.61 (Note 5) + 2,500.00 + 291.55 = £4,485.16

(3)   5,985.74 – 4,485.16 = £1,500.58

Notes

(1)   The basic tax point for goods is the date on which they were collected, delivered or made available to the customer. However if a payment is received before the basic tax point then the date of payment is the date that the supply is treated as taking place.

(2)   Output VAT

	Net	VAT
	£	£
Mr Wilson	80.00	14.00
Mrs Jepson	6,580.00	1,151.50
Mr Wilson	2,820.00	493.50
Ms Clancy	9,295.62	1,626.74
	———	———
	18,775.62	3,285.74
	———	———

(3)   Input VAT

	Net	VAT
	£	£
Magnum Kitchens	4,900.00	857.50
Ellse Electricals	827.00	141.83
Ellse Electricals	67.32	11.78
Nicholas Baines	3,900.00	682.50
	———	———
Deductible input tax	9,694.32	1,693.61
Broken Heart (non-deductible expense)	117.00	20.48
	———	———
	9,811.32	1,714.09
	———	———

(4)   Only the debt of £1,957.55 (including VAT) from Mrs P Taylor-Young qualifies for bad debt relief for VAT as in order to qualify for the relief at least six months must have elapsed from the due date for the payment of the supply. Therefore the VAT on this debt £291.55 (£1,957.55 × 7/47) is included in the output tax shown in Box 4 of the VAT return.

VAT account

	£		£
Input VAT		Output VAT	
VAT on purchases	1,693.61	VAT on sales	3,285.74
Understatement of input		Understatement of output	
tax from previous returns	2,500.00	tax from previous returns	2,700.00
Bad debt relief	291.55		
Payable to Customs			
& Excise	1,500.58		
	———		———
	5,985.74		5,985.74
	———		———

TASK 2

MEMORANDUM

To: Jean Simons

From: The bookkeeper

Date: 2 November 20X7

Subject: Customs and Excise control visits

Control visits

As VAT is a self-assessed tax it is understandable that Customs and Excise would wish to carry out spot checks to ensure that businesses are accounting correctly for VAT. These spot checks are known as control visits.

The purpose of the visit for the Customs and Excise officer is to ensure that VAT returns have been correctly filled out by reference to the original VAT records. These visits are also designed as a deterrent to fraud.

Such visits are also an ideal opportunity for you to sort out any difficulties that you feel have occurred in practice.

Assessments

If the officer feels that VAT returns have been incorrectly made then an assessment can be issued for the additional amount to be paid or repaid. Such an assessment must be made within two years of the end of the accounting period to which it relates or within one year of the necessary evidence becoming available to the officer. This is all subject to an overriding time limit of three years or twenty years if fraud or dishonest conduct is involved.

FOULKS LYNCH
PUBLICATIONS

TASK 3

MEMORANDUM

To: Jean Simons

From: The Bookkeeper

Date: 8 November 20X7

Subject: Your queries

1   There are two types of supply of goods and services for VAT purposes. These are exempt supplies and taxable supplies. Exempt supplies are not subject to VAT. Taxable supplies may be standard rated, taxed at the standard rate of 17.5%, or zero rated, taxed at a rate of 0%.

2   If you were to make zero rated supplies then this would not affect the input VAT that you could reclaim from Customs & Excise. All deductible input tax could still be reclaimed.

However if you were to make exempt supplies as well as standard and/or zero rated supplies then you would be known as a partially exempt trader. For such a trader the VAT on inputs can only be recovered to the extent that they are deemed to relate to the taxable supplies that you make. The VAT on inputs that relate to exempt supplies made is not recoverable.

3   If a credit note is to be valid documentation for VAT purposes then it must refer to the original invoice for the goods by number and date and the reason for the credit note being issued must be stated.

4   If the total value of the goods purchased, including VAT, is less than £100 then an invoice which shows only the VAT inclusive figure will be valid provided that the invoice also includes the supplier's name, address, VAT registration number, the date of supply, description of the goods and the rate of VAT applicable.

However if the VAT inclusive amount is greater than £100 then this will not be a valid invoice with which to support a claim for input VAT and a full VAT invoice must be requested.

ANSWERS TO PRACTICE SIMULATION 5

TASK 1

Sales to external customers

Manufacturing and Sales Divisions combined

	Monthly totals £000	Cumulative total for the year £000
20X3		
January	452	452
February	317	769
March	264	1,033
April	365	1,398
May	413	1,811
June	310	2,121
July	284	2,405
August	385	2,790
September	326	3,116
October	325	3,441
November	286	3,727
December	454	4,181
20X4		
January	448	448
February	281	729
March	283	1,012
April	404	1,416
May	388	1,804
June	352	2,156
July	273	2,429
August	433	2,862
September	418	3,280
October	365	3,645
November	325	3,970
December	341	4,311

TASK 2

Cumulative external sales 20X3 and 20X4

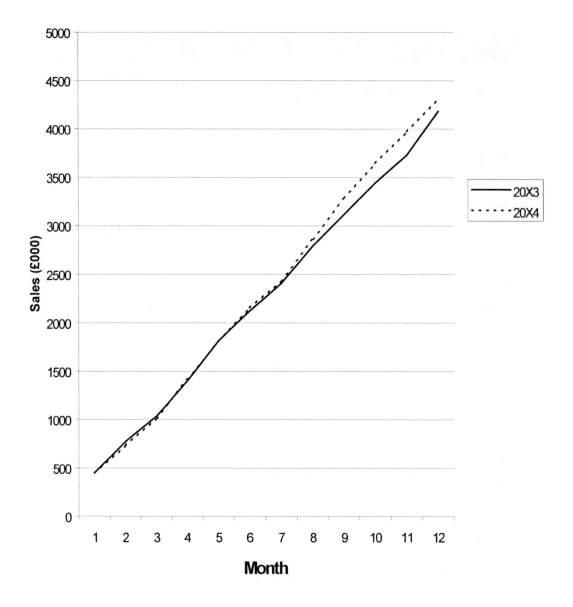

TASK 3

Indexed sales to external customers

Manufacturing and Sales Divisions combined

	Unadjusted totals £000	Index factor	Indexed totals £000
20X4			
January	448	100/111.6	401
February	281	100/112.2	250
March	283	100/113.0	250
April	404	100/113.8	355
May	388	100/114.4	339
June	352	100/114.9	306
July	273	100/115.7	236
August	433	100/116.3	372
September	418	100/117.0	357
October	365	100/117.5	311
November	325	100/118.1	275
December	341	100/118.9	287

Notes

1. In the first column, insert the monthly totals of external sales calculated in Task 1.

2. In the second column, insert the index factor required to convert to January 20X0 values.

Note: The index for January 20X0 is 100. To convert figures in other months to January 20X0 values, we have to multiply by a factor 100/month's index.

3. In the third column, calculate the monthly sales in January 20X0 terms (to the nearest £1,000).

TASK 4

MANUFACTURERS AND PRODUCERS ASSOCIATION

17 Pharaoh Street, Gadtown GW3 1QR

Dear Member

Please supply the following information for your most recent accounting period.

The information should be prepared in accordance with the notes below.

Name of company	Jacob Limited
Membership number	225671
Financial year end	31 December 20X4
1 Turnover for the year	£4,311,000
Percentage change on previous year (+/-)	+ 3.11%
2 Production costs as percentage of sales	59.85%
3 Administration costs as percentage of sales	15.66%
4 Distribution costs as percentage of sales	11.85%
5 Gross profit percentage	40.15%
6 Net profit percentage	8.56%
7 Return on capital employed	4.76%

Notes

1.   Turnover should be stated net of VAT.

2.   Return on capital employed should be calculated as the proportion of net profit to total capital employed, expressed as a percentage.

3.   Percentages and ratios should be stated to two decimal places.

Please return the completed form to Leah Laban at the above address by 31 January 20X5.

Thank you for your assistance.

Workings:

1   Increase in sales in 20X4 = (in £000) 4,311 – 4,181 = 130.

     Percentage increase in sales turnover = (311/4,181) x 100% = 3.11%.

2   Production costs as a percentage of sales = (2,580/4,311) x 100% = 59.85%.

3   Administration costs as a percentage of sales = (675/4,311) x 100% = 15.66%.

4   Distribution costs as a percentage of sales = (511/4,311) x 100% = 11.85%.

5   Gross profit percentage = (1,731/4,311) x 100% = 40.15%.

6   Net profit percentage = (369/4,311) x 100% = 8.56%.

7   Return on capital employed = (369/7,748) x 100% = 4.76%.

TASK 5

MEMO

To: Dan Asher

From: Vinny Taswell

Date: 15 January 20X5

Subject: **Ratios and performance indicators for 20X4**

I have calculated the statistics for 20X4 that you asked for.

1.   The **gross profit percentage** is 40.15%. This has fallen from 44.10% in 20X3. This could be due to an increase in production costs (see point 3 below).

2.   The **net profit percentage** is 8.56%. This has risen from 8.01% the previous year, in spite of the fall in gross profit percentage. This is probably due to good control over administration and distribution costs.

3.   The **production cost per unit**. Production costs in 20X4 were £2,580,000 and we produced 168,000 Benjis, giving a production cost per unit of £15.36. This has risen from £14.50 in 20X3. I do not have inflation to indicate why production costs per unit have risen, but higher materials costs or direct labour costs, or possibly a higher overhead cost per unit, could be the reason.

4.   The **value of sales earned per employee** is £32,171.64. This has fallen from £32,946.25 in 20X3. Total sales turnover rose by 3.11% in 20X4, which means that the total number of employees must have risen by more than this percentage amount. As a result, productivity of the work force appears to have fallen.

On a separate issue, I have attached a completed annual return for 20X4 for the Manufacturers and Producers Association, for your approval and authorisation before sending it to the Association. The Association would like us to submit the completed return by 31 January.

Workings:

Value of sales earned per employee   =   £4,311,000/134

                                          =   £32,171.64

HM Customs and Excise

Value Added Tax Return
For the period
01–10–X4 **to** 31–12–X4

For Official Use

Registration number	Period
570 4060 19	12 X4

┌   ┐

JACOB LIMITED
UNIT 7
THAMESVIEW BUSINESS PARK
CULTHAM
CM5 8RW

└   ┘

You could be liable to a financial penalty if your completed return and all the VAT payable are not received by the due date.

Due date: 31.01.X5

For official use D O R only	

Fold | Here

Before you fill in this form please read the notes on the back and the VAT leaflet *"Filling in your VAT return"*. Fill all boxes clearly in ink, and write 'none' where necessary. Don't put a dash or leave any box blank. If there are no pence write "00" in the pence column. Do **not** enter more than one amount in any box.

For official use			£	p
VAT due in this period on **sales** and other outputs	**1**		164,925	09
VAT due in this period on **acquisitions** from other **EC Member States**	**2**		NONE	
Total VAT due (**the sum of boxes 1 and 2**)	**3**		164,925	09
VAT reclaimed in this period on **purchases** and other inputs (including acquisitions from the EC)	**4**		100,448	53
Net VAT to be paid to Customs or reclaimed by you (**Difference between boxes 3 and 4**)	**5**		64,476	56
Total value of **sales** and all other outputs excluding any VAT. **Include your box 8 figure**	**6**		1,031,009	00
Total value of **purchases** and all other inputs excluding any VAT. **Include your box 9 figure**	**7**		612,206	00
Total value of **all supplies** of goods and related services, excluding any VAT, to other **EC Member States**	**8**		88,579	00
Total value of all **acquisitions** of goods and related services, excluding any VAT, from other **EC Member States**	**9**		NONE	00

If you are enclosing a payment please tick this box	DECLARATION: You, or someone on your behalf, must sign below.
3	I, ... *DAN ASHER* .... declare that the (Full name of signatory in BLOCK LETTERS) information given above is true and complete. Signature .... Date .... **A false declaration can result in prosecution**

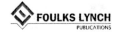

TASK 7

JACOB LIMITED
Unit 7, Thamesview Business Park, Cultham CM5 8RW

15 January 20X5

H M Customs and Excise
29 Parson Street
Cultham
CM1 6TY

Dear Sir/Madam

VAT Registration number 578 4060 19

My company is a manufacturing company, and we are thinking of extending our business activities to include the offer of product warranties to customers buying our product. I am writing to ask whether the warrants would be an exempt supply or a taxable supply for VAT purposes.

I should be grateful for any information you can provide on this matter, and in particular I should be grateful if you could send me a copy of any of your publications that deals with VAT and the supply of product warranties.

Yours faithfully

Dan Asher

ACCOUNTANT

TASK 8

<table>
<tr><td colspan="2" align="center">**MEMO**</td></tr>
<tr><td>To:</td><td>Dan Asher</td></tr>
<tr><td>From:</td><td>Vinny Taswell</td></tr>
<tr><td>Date:</td><td>15 January 20X5</td></tr>
<tr><td>Subject:</td><td>VAT – exempt supplies</td></tr>
</table>

I enclose a draft letter to the local VAT office asking for information about VAT on product warranties and a copy of any publication on this topic.

If you are correct in believing that the warranties will be an exempt supply, we would be selling a mixture of taxable and exempt supplies in our business when we start to sell the warrants. The basic rule is that when a business sells a mix of taxable and exempt supplies, input VAT can be recovered only in relation to the taxable supplies and cannot be recovered in relation to the exempt supplies.

However, if sales of exempt supplies are only a small proportion of total sales, a business can recover all its input tax. I can obtain more details about this from the VAT office, if you want me to.

ANSWERS TO PRACTICE SIMULATION 6

TASK 1

Total production cost per unit of finished goods transferred from Assembly to Sales and Administration in year ended 31 December 20X3.

£
13,769

Ratio of total factory overheads to total factory labour cost in year ended 31 December 20X3

0.89

Workings
1. Production cost per unit of finished goods = £715,986 ÷ 52.
2. Ratio of factory overheads to factory labour cost:

$$\frac{£(88,903+126,732)}{£(124,561+117,410)}$$

TASK 2

Albion Manufacturing Limited
Consolidated Statement of Costs and Revenues
for the year ended 31 December 20X3

		20X3
	£	£
Sales		1,452,317
Cost of sales		
Materials	258,380	
Factory labour	241,971	
Factory overhead	215,635	
Movement in stock of finished goods	12,469	
		728,455
Gross profit		723,862
Sales and administration salaries	207,514	
Other admin and establishment costs	247,091	
		454,605
Net profit before taxation		269,257

Consolidated Statement of Costs and Revenues
for the year ended 31 December 2001

	Unadjusted	Adjusted
	£	£
Sales	1,304,723	1,369,959
Cost of sales		
Materials	248,501	258,441
Factory labour	239,550	246,737
Factory overhead	213,452	219,856
Movement in stock of finished goods	(13,761)	(13,761)
	687,742	711,273
Gross profit	616,981	658,686
Sales and administration salaries	199,502	207,482
Other admin and establishment costs	228,787	237,938
	428,289	445,420
Net profit before taxation	188,692	213,266

TASK 3

Percentage Increase/Decrease in 20X3 compared with 20X2

	20X3	20X2 (adjusted)	Percentage increase/(decrease)
	£	£	%
Sales	1,452,317	1,369,959	6.01
Cost of sales	728,455	711,273	2.42
Net profit	269,257	213,266	26.25

TASK 4

MEMORANDUM

To: Amanda Buckley

From: Accounts Clerk

Date: 19 January 20X4

Subject: Results for 20X3

In reply to your memo of 17 January, here are my findings. Note that all comparisons with 20X2 refer to the adjusted figures for that year.

Sales are up by 6.01% from £1,369,959 to £1,452,317.

Factory cost of sales is down from 51.92% of sales to 50.16%. Accounting for this there are slight decreases in percentage terms in the cost of materials, factory labour and factory overhead, despite the increase in sales volume. The full significance of this is not quite clear from the figures I have so far, because it appears that production volume was lower this year than last (finished goods stock declined by £12,469 over the year). This could be an area you might want to look at.

Sales and administration salaries are virtually unchanged despite the increase in sales volume.

Other admin and establishment costs are up by 3.85%.

As a result of all this net profit in 20X3 amounts to 18.54% of sales, compared to 15.57% in 20X2.

I hope this is what you need for your paper, but please get back to me if there is anything more I can do.

You also asked for bar charts to illustrate the results in 20X2 and 20X3; see the sheet attached.

Regards,

Signature

TASK 5

Financial Information in Support of Application

(extracts)

Name of company....*Albion Manufacturing Limited*..............

Year ended............*31 Dec 20X3*...................................

Data...

	Current year		Previous year	
	£%	of sales	£%	of sales
Sales	1,452,317	100.00	1,304,723	100.00
Gross profit	723,862	49.84	616,981	47.29
Net profit before taxation	269,257	18.54	188,692	14.46
Total labour and salary costs (A)	449,485	30.95	439,052	33.65
Production costs not included in (A)	486,484	33.50	448,192	34.35
Other costs	247,091	17.01	228,787	17.54

TASK 6

MEMO
To: Amanda Buckley
From: Accounting technician
Date: XXXXXX
Subject: Grant application
I have completed the form asking for financial information in support of the application for a grant.
Could you please authorise me to send the form to John Kay, who is responsible for making the application to the grant authority.

FOULKS LYNCH
PUBLICATIONS

AAT Order Form

4 The Griffin Centre, Staines Road, Feltham, Middlesex, TW14 0HS, UK.
Tel: +44 (0) 20 8831 9990 Fax: + 44 (0) 20 8831 9991
Order online: www.foulkslynch.com Email: sales@ewfl-global.com

For assessments in 2003/2004		Textbooks		Workbooks		Combined Textbooks/ Workbooks	
Foundation stage – NVQ/SVQ 2							
1 & 2	Receipts and Payments	£10.95	☐	£10.95	☐		
3	Preparing Ledger Balances and an Initial Trial Balance	£10.95	☐	£10.95	☐		
4	Supplying Information for Management Control					£10.95	☐
21*	Working with Computers					£10.95	☐
22 & 23#	Achieving Personal Effectiveness and Health & Safety					£10.95	☐
Intermediate stage – NVQ/SVQ 3							
5	Maintaining Financial Records and Preparing Accounts	£10.95	☐	£10.95	☐		
6	Recording and Evaluating Cost and Revenue	£10.95	☐	£10.95	☐		
7	Preparing Reports and Returns	£10.95	☐	£10.95	☐		
8 & 9	Performance Management, Value Enhancement and Resource Planning and Control	£10.95	☐	£10.95	☐		
Technician stage – NVQ/SVQ 4							
10	Managing Systems and People in the Accounting Environment	£10.95	☐	£10.95	☐		
11	Preparing Financial Statements	£10.95	☐	£10.95	☐		
15	Cash Management and Credit Control	£10.95	☐	£10.95	☐		
17	Implementing Auditing Procedures	£10.95	☐	£10.95	☐		
18	Business Taxation FA 2003	£10.95	☐	£10.95	☐		
19	Personal Taxation FA 2003	£10.95	☐	£10.95	☐		

* Unit 21 can be taken at Foundation Level or Intermediate Level

Unit 23 can be taken at any level

Postage, Packaging and Delivery (Per Item):

	First	Each Extra
UK	£5.00	£2.00
Europe (incl ROI and CI)	£7.00	£4.00
Rest of World	£22.00	£8.00

Product Sub Total £..................	Post & Packaging £..................	Order Total £....................	(Payments in UK £ Sterling)

Customer Details

☐ Mr ☐ Mrs ☐ Ms ☐ Miss Other ....

Initials:................................. Surname: ....

Address: ....

....

....

Postcode: ....

Telephone: ....

Email: ....

Fax: ....

Delivery Address – if different from above

Address: ....

....

Postcode: ....

Telephone: ....

Payment

1   I enclose Cheque/PO/Bankers Draft for £....................................

    Please make cheques payable to '**Foulks Lynch**'.

2   Charge MasterCard/Visa/Switch a/c no:

Valid from: ☐☐☐   Expiry date: ☐☐

Issue No: (Switch only)

Signature: .... Date: ....

Declaration

I agree to pay as indicated on this form and understand that
Foulks Lynch Terms and Conditions apply (available on request).

Signature: .... Date: ....

Notes: Prices are correct at time of going to print but are subject to change

---

Delivery – United Kingdom – 5 working days
please Eire & EU Countries – 10 working days
allow: Rest of World – 10 working days

Notes: All orders over 1kg will be fully tracked & insured.
Signature required on receipt of order. Delivery times
subject to stock availability.

FOULKS LYNCH
PUBLICATIONS